DISCIPLINE WITH DIGNITY FOR CHALLENGING YOUTH

ALLEN N. MENDLER
RICHARD L. CURWIN

NATIONAL EDUCATIONAL SERVICE
BLOOMINGTON, INDIANA   1999

Cover design by Bill Dillon

Printed in the United States of America

Printed on recycled paper

ISBN 1-879639-65-3

Dedication

TO THE MEMORY OF Bernard Klein, my father-in-law, for the precious gifts of love and devotion to his children and grandchildren. He taught me by example that at the end of the day it is connection to family, friends, and community that defines a truly successful man.

Allen N. Mendler

Rochester, New York

To Yocheved Chana and Betzalel Ze'ev Curwin, my grandchildren, for their eagerness to explore, consuming desire to learn everything, joyful spirits, and especially for continuing to remind me of the wonder of children.

Richard L. Curwin

San Francisco, California

Acknowledgments

WE WANT TO THANK the many thousands of committed educators who, along with us, continue to use, develop, and re-invent effective methods of discipline that teach responsibility while providing the kind of climate that enables even difficult students to learn. In particular, we wish to acknowledge the following people for their support of our work and for their assistance in helping us become better thinkers, presenters, writers, and people:

Barbara Mendler, for her love and for her excellence as an educator.

Lisa Mendler, for the sacrifices she makes in understanding that her Dad needs to be away from home more than they both like so that educators and children can benefit from his work.

Mark Goldberg, for his many rich editorial contributions, his generous help and support, and his friendship.

Frank Koontz, Rich Herzberg, and staff at the Bureau of Education and Research, for their lengthy support of our work and the many helpful suggestions they have given over the years to help us convey our knowledge successfully.

Jeff Jones, Julia Hunt, Colette Richardson, Alan Blankstein, Rhonda Rieseberg, and the staff at the National Educational Service for their many years of support and sponsorship.

David and Colleen Zawadzki, outstanding educators in Syracuse, New York, and Discipline with Dignity trainers, who have greatly contributed to proving that Discipline with Dignity can be as effective with urban youth as with other youth.

Debra Keller, who set up the Discipline with Dignity program in Cozad, Nebraska.

Nancy Modrak, book editor at ASCD.

Phil Harris, professional development coordinator at Phi Delta Kappa, for his love of kids and commitment to creating programs that enrich their lives.

Arnie Prockott at the National Educational Institute.

Larry Brendtro and the staff and faculty of the Black Hills seminars.

Mary Ann Bider of the Learning Institute.

Elizabeth Osta, of the Rochester city schools, for her boundless energy and creativity.

Mrs. Meike, principal, and all the teachers and staff of Richard Edwards Elementary school in Chicago.

The many students who took the Discipline with Dignity course at St. Mary's College in Moraga, California.

All the students who contributed excellent projects from the Discipline with Dignity courses at the University of Vermont in Burlington, Vermont.

Edna Olive-Jones, principal, and her school, the Florence Bertell Academy.

Our many fine trainers associated with the Teacher Education Institute and those affiliated with the New York State United Teachers.

Jerry Evanski, Wiletta Corbett, and Susan Strauss, who have so competently provided our training to educators throughout the country.

Tammy Rowland, our faithful and tireless program manager, who keeps the organization running.

Contents

About the Authors

ALLEN N. MENDLER, PH.D., is an educator, school psychologist, and the parent of three children. He has worked extensively with children of all ages, with an emphasis on developing effective strategies for educators and youth professionals to help challenging students succeed. As one of the internationally recognized authors of *Discipline with Dignity*, Dr. Mendler has given thousands of workshops throughout the United States and internationally, and is highly acclaimed as a keynote speaker and presenter for numerous educational organizations.

Dr. Mendler is the author or co-author of several books, including *As Tough as Necessary, What Do I Do When...? How to Achieve Discipline with Dignity in the Classroom,* and *Power Struggles: Effective Methods for Educators.* His articles have appeared in many journals, including *Educational Leadership, Parenting,* and *Reaching Today's Youth.* He lives with his family in Rochester, New York.

Richard L. Curwin, Ed.D., is known internationally for providing thousands of educators and parents with practical, proven ideas to effectively manage children's behavior in a manner that respects the dignity of each individual. Dr. Curwin is co-author of the acclaimed book *Discipline with Dignity*, and author of *Rediscovering Hope: Our Greatest Teaching Strategy*. His most recent publication, *As Tough as Necessary*, addresses the problems of hostility, aggression, and violence in our schools. His articles have appeared in *Instructor, Learning,* and *Educational Leadership*.

Dr. Curwin has been an assistant professor of education at San Francisco State University, has taught junior high school, and has conducted workshops for over 15 years.

Preface

WHEN WE WERE ASKED to write a new book on discipline, one focusing on "challenging" children, we went through a long internal process of reflection. What have we learned that is new? What could we share that has not already been shared? Do we know more strategies and methods? Are there new frameworks, organizing concepts, or structures? Have our fundamental beliefs changed in a substantial way? How have we changed?

When we tried to answer these and other questions, the word that reappeared most often was *change*. We came to understand that the most significant and important issue was change itself. We wanted to share how our approach to discipline has changed and how we believe schools and educators must change in order to create change in our most challenging students, those who are most resistant to change.

Our fundamental beliefs have remained the same over the years. We believe that:

- Schools are for children, not the staff, teachers, and administrators who work there.

- Students must always be treated with dignity.

- Teaching students how to be responsible should be the core of any discipline program.

- All students are equally important, even the most difficult ones.

Even though our principles have remained unchanged, the way we apply them has evolved over the years. For example, we once rejected punishments as theoretically incompatible with dignity and useless as a practical strategy. We have found, however, that punishments can help as a deterrent with the small percentage of children who might cross the line into dangerous behavior without them. Readers who are familiar with our Discipline with Dignity approach will find other, similar adjustments in our writing.

Discipline with Dignity for Challenging Youth offers a number of new concepts and strategies that have evolved from our efforts to find better ways to help educators assist their most challenging students. These include:

- The difference between effort and achievement

- Three types of interventions

- Threat versus challenge

- Seven goals for successful discipline

- Strategies for fighting faculty resistance

- Strategies for fighting student resistance

- Strategies for fighting resistance within ourselves

Although this book contains dozens of new strategies that we have gathered from successful schools, great teachers, and our own creativity, it is not merely a how-to book that lists one technique after another. Each strategy is thoroughly explained in context, so you will not only know what to do, but also understand why you need to do it.

Perhaps the most important thing we realized is that change is a natural part of life. Growth through change is not only necessary but also inevitable in our fast-moving world. Change can still be painful, difficult, and destabilizing. Nevertheless, as long as our students and their home lives, needs, and fears change, we must change too.

1

Introduction

How we treat our best students shows our aspirations; how we treat our most challenging students shows our values.

CHALLENGING STUDENTS ARE hard to influence and harder to change. Rules mean little to these students. Rewards and punishments may have temporary, positive results but they eventually lose their effectiveness. Even consequences that can teach better behavior are often ineffective. Most "enlightened" programs for difficult students include social skills training, conflict-resolution approaches, stress-reduction practices, and the educational curriculum. Yet, too often, these programs and the well-intentioned professionals who administer them fail because the programs have been created with minimal, if any, input from the youth they are designed to help. Even when a program's success is achieved in alternative settings, its components are rarely extended beyond those special settings. Mainstream programs seldom have the resources, teacher expertise, time, or commitment to implement similar components. Another obstacle to success is an underlying belief that especially difficult students should fit in a system that is "good enough" for everyone else. In some ways, it is easier and more practical to label, do daily battle with, and remove undesirable students.

Unfortunately, one of the hardest parts of being a teacher is not knowing how well we are doing. People in almost every other profession quickly know if their work has been successful. If you are a baseball player, you get a hit or you strike out. If you are a surgeon, the patient lives or dies. If you are a lawyer, you win or lose a case. If you are an engineer, the bridge you designed either stands or collapses. The results in these professions are concrete. But teaching is different. Although educators have a number of assessment tools that measure short-term, academic progress, we do not know if our efforts will succeed in the long term. Everything we do is based on faith. We do not know for sure that the assignments we give or the behavioral interventions we use make any difference in the lives of our students. This uncertainty makes us constantly wonder, "Am I doing this the best way?"

CLIMBING THE MOUNTAIN

Imagine that one summer you decide to try mountain climbing, an activity in which you always know where you stand, quite literally. You train for it, study for it, and even find a mountain-climbing website on the Internet where you can practice virtual mountain climbing when your legs are tired. The big day finally comes. You fly to Arizona, pick the most beautiful mountain you can find, and start climbing. About halfway through the climb, you assess your situation. You're feeling very good! You are succeeding. All of your training is paying off. Several hours into the climb, however, things change. The climbing becomes more difficult, stressful, and dangerous. You are tired, thirsty, and hot. Your legs are getting a bit wobbly. You have a near fall where you could have hurt yourself or worse. You keep going, and eventually, with great perseverance and effort, you get to the top. It wasn't easy.

When you get there, you are overwhelmed with two powerful feelings. The first is relief ("Phew, I did it"), and the second is exhilaration ("I did it, I did it!"). As you look around the top of the mountain and enjoy the panoramic view while savoring your conquest, you notice something very unusual on the other side: there is an escalator ferrying tourists from the desert floor to the mountain top where you stand. You realize that you could have taken the escalator and been at the top in 15 minutes. You could have even enjoyed a croissant and a cappuccino during the ascent. You could have worn sneakers, high heels, sandals, or no shoes at all. It would not have mattered. After you finish admiring the view, you take the escalator down the mountain. As you walk back to your hotel, you meet a friend who tells you that he wants to climb the same mountain. Here is the question:

Do you tell your friend about the escalator?

THE DILEMMA: "ELBOW GREASE" OR THE EASY WAY?

This question helps us focus on the advantages and disadvantages of struggle and mastery. Western society increasingly prefers taking the escalator over climbing the mountain. This "fast and easy" standard has affected the way we live, the way we teach, and the way we discipline.

More and more people today have come to expect that their needs, wants, and desires will be met quickly and painlessly.

There is little tolerance for boredom and delayed gratification. Fast and easy have become the catchwords for most advertising. Those in media programming and politics can gauge their success with immediate rating systems and polls. Technological advances have led to products designed to make our lives easier and to help us respond to life's demands more quickly. Consumer frustration with having to wait even a few seconds to access computerized information now leads to pressure on the computer industry to make future computers that provide information even more quickly.

Are children not working as hard today as they were five years ago? Have we convinced our children that fast and easy is better? Do American children believe work has value? Many educators become exasperated as they wonder how to motivate their students to work. Getting students to do their homework, their schoolwork, or even to make an effort has become more difficult because an *easier* life has become more highly valued than a challenging life. Role models like ballplayers who do not hustle and are offered millions but refuse the contract because it is not enough money to *play a game* convince children that hard work has little payoff. When children see their role models assuming this attitude, all they see is the athlete's apparent reluctance to work hard. They do not understand how hard the athlete had to work to get to the level where he or she could choose to slack off and still be in demand. Sadly, the message is, "You don't need to do more hard work. You need to get a good agent."

FAST AND EASY EDUCATION

American education is succumbing to the lure of "fast and easy" in two ways. First of all, what we measure, value, and reward is often based on appearances, which can be illusions. Since it is easier to measure achievement than effort, we create and exalt revised versions of standardized tests that often yield little more than the illusion of success. Schools seek opportunities to proudly display their students' successes at or above grade level. Grades, honor rolls, and reward and point systems generally value achievement rather than effort. While such measures can yield useful information, they are too often used because they are easy to quantify and understand. Unfortunately, there is little assurance that test results reflect any more than the amount of class time spent practicing taking the tests. We believe that measuring how high students climb is not as important as measuring their effort while they climb.

The importance of effort is understood by good coaches, who know their teams are not good or bad based on the number of victories but rather by the effort the team makes while training and competing. When coaches focus on effort, they emphasize the value of doing one's best over innate ability and praise players who work hard to improve their skills. This praise tells players that their efforts matter and encourages them to try even harder. What works on the gym floor also works in the classroom. Do you have students who get As without trying? Do you have students who get the lowest grades but still try hard? What do each of these groups learn from their grades about the value of their efforts? The answer is obvious: there isn't any.

Some children do not learn by being compared with others or by being pushed artificially to achieve. Because their efforts are not reflected in their grades, they shut down and stop trying. Some of these children create behavior problems to conceal their real concerns. Because it feels better to be labeled "bad" than "stupid," many children who have trouble with learning will also challenge us behaviorally. If they are bad at being good, they reason, they can always be good at being bad.

The second way that American education is succumbing to "fast and easy" is in our choice of discipline methods when rules are broken. Too many of our strategies and programs for managing behavior are based on the "easy" escalator approach. Examples include efforts to reduce and simplify discipline codes with such strategies as zero tolerance, sequential consequences (i.e., the first offense results in a reminder; the second offense results in detention, etc.), and other punishments or conse-quences administered without regard to their instructional value. But for troubled children to change, they need time with patient, caring adults who understand that using methods that bring about change over time is probably going to be the best way.

Our most difficult students cannot be reached through threats. Because they have often lacked love, limits, and support from the important adults in their lives, they have learned not to care. You say to them, "I'm going to call your mother." And they say,

"So who cares? Call her."

"We don't have a telephone."

"I hope you find her. I haven't seen her in months."

"She's going to be here tomorrow with her boyfriend to get you."

Escalator discipline relies primarily on threat or reward. It is based on the misguided belief that if the consequence or reward is severe or pleasant enough, the student will generally comply with the rules. But when threats and rewards do not work—and they rarely do over the long term—escalator disci-pline leads to the removal of students from their class or school. This approach is not a good choice unless the safety of other students is involved. We may be able to remove difficult students from our class, but we cannot remove them from our lives. When they are not in school, they may be bothering shoppers at the mall, robbing our houses while we teach, or joining gangs. Later, they may fill our prisons, welfare rolls, and homeless shelters. Too often, they become drug abusers, spousal abusers, and child abusers. It is sobering to note that we have more prisoners than graduate students in America.

FIVE PRINCIPLES FOR EDUCATORS

We may not be able to reach them all, but as professional educators we should not pick and choose who will survive and who will flourish. Those decisions are best left to the courts and criminal justice systems. Our job is to teach. When a student behaves poorly, we are responsible for teaching him or her a better way to handle the situation. Five basic principles provide the foundation for the many discipline strategies in this book. These principles are based on our responsibility as educators to teach alternative behaviors.

Principle 1: We are responsible for teaching all students. In a society that risks losing its freedoms because we fear for our safety (Curwin & Mendler, 1997), we will reach a point at which the emotional and economic costs of institutionalizing our youth will overwhelm us. We may already be there! It costs $32,000 to send someone to prison for a year, but only $6,000 a year on average to educate one student in public school. It is even cheaper to send someone to Harvard than to prison. If we fail to reach, educate, and give our students the tools they need to master social skills, they will hurt us and are likely to continue hurting others. Although we cannot choose who we teach, and we may not be able to reach all of our students, we must never judge who is worth our effort and who is not. Our job as professional educators is to treat all students as if they are worthy and capable.

We cannot change children in a positive manner by throwing them away. The only way to change children is by bringing them closer to us. We must make them part of our group because when they are not, there is no incentive for them to follow our rules. Most disruptive youth are seeking structure and limits. If they do not find them at school, they will look to gangs, cults, or drug lords who have strict codes and a clear hierarchy. The best solution we have for disruptive youth begins by keeping them within the school's structured environment. Then we need to help them do better in that environment by providing them with the resources and supports they need to learn new social skills that will lead to better choices.

Principle 2: View difficult behavior as opportunities to educate for change; reserve *leverage* for excessively disruptive or dangerous situations. We have found that you do not change people by hurting them. Instead, you influence change by giving them the skills they need in a welcoming, appealing way that helps them see how these skills will actually improve their lives. Unless students understand how coming to class, doing their work, and behaving well benefits them, they are unlikely to meet these expectations. A professional educator views this change process as a mountain climb with an escalator available for when speed is more important than the quality of experience. This book focuses on *educating* for change and saving *leverage*—threat, reward, and punishment—for those few situations when someone may hurt him- or herself or others.

Principle 3: The more we motivate, the less we discipline. When one of our sons was in first grade, he came home from school one day in a stubborn mood.

"Daddy," he said, "I have homework and I'm not going to do it, and you can't make me. I'm going to watch television."

I said, "Danny, tell me what your homework is."

"No, I'm not telling."

"Why?"

"I don't want you to trick me into doing it."

"Danny, I work with first-grade teachers. The more I know about what they do, the better I can do my job. And if I do my job really well, I'll make more money so I can buy a better television set." The good thing about stubborn first-graders is that you can occasionally trick them.

"Okay, I'll tell you what it is, but I'm not doing it. I have four vocabulary words, and they're all stupid. And I have to write a sentence about every one of them, and I'm not writing dumb sentences about these dumb words."

"What's the first word?"

"It's a dumb, stupid box."

And I said, "I know why you don't want to write a sentence about a box. Nobody told you it was a magic box."

"What's magic about it?"

"I'm not telling, and you can't make me," I replied.

"That's not fair. I told you what it was."

I said, "I'll make a deal with you. If you tell me how big it is, I'll tell you how it's magic."

He closed his eyes and said, "I know how big it is. It's this big." And moving his arms, he made the biggest box he could make.

"What color is it?" I asked.

He closed his eyes again and asked, "Is it red?" I said, "Don't ask, Danny. You tell."

"It's red."

And we kept doing this. It turned out to be the bicycle he wants to get for his next present. So he wrote on his paper, "My magic box has a big red bicycle." He liked doing this so much that he wrote four more sentences about the box on his paper. I had to trick him to get him to stop.

The example above shows how challenge works better than threat. Every good coach knows this. A threat might have produced a paper with words on it, but little would have been learned except to write quickly so more television could be watched. It takes effort to find the right challenge for a child, but so does finding out what a student fears so you can threaten him or her into better behavior with it. Most school-based threats are useless because the student has no fear of what we threaten to do. They do not care if they get another detention or call home if these punishments have often been used in the past. For many students, no threat can compete with the fear of their lives at home.

Principle 4: Discipline is just another form of instruction. The primary goal of a discipline method is to teach better behavior. Although punishment or reward may be a byproduct, the major questions an educator needs to ask are, "How is this method going to improve behavior?" and "What is the student likely to learn?" If teaching improved behavior is our goal, then we must be prepared to match the method to the student in a manner that differs little from conventional instructional practices. High schools often have different levels of instruction. Elementary school teachers regularly have multiple reading or math groups to reflect academic and cognitive diversity. All schools recognize the value of individual educational plans (IEPs) for academically challenged students. We must also recognize behavioral diversity by providing individualized prevention or intervention methods that help teach improved and acceptable behavior. As we have previously discussed in depth

(Curwin, 1992; Curwin & Mendler, 1988; Mendler, 1992), we will be more successful when we focus on being fair rather than on treating everyone in the same way. Effective discipline that teaches responsibility focuses on giving each student what he or she needs to succeed, not on treating all students equally.

Principle 5: Have numerous strategies and lots of heart for success. When our goal is to teach rather than punish, we will need a number of strategies. Because learning is influenced by many factors, there are many things that can be done to prevent discipline problems from occurring and to intervene successfully when things become difficult. While there is no one-size-fits-all strategy and no Holy Grail approach, several structures and frameworks can help us successfully work with behaviorally diverse and disruptive youth.

Educators who want to work successfully with challenging youth also need an endless amount of patience and caring. The fact is that students are becoming more disruptive at younger ages. They are doing more insidious things and often lack remorse (Curwin & Mendler, 1997). Not only must we love the learning process so that we can convey that love to our students, we must also love *who* they are even if we do not always appreciate *what* they do.

Like all worthy challenges, successful discipline is rarely fast or easy. But its rewards can be very gratifying when we see our students improving their lives by changing their behavior for the better, and for good.

2

The First "R"

Discipline is less about punishing and more about teaching responsibility.

THE PURPOSE OF SCHOOL HAS been defined in many ways. School prepares students for college, jobs, and citizenship. School keeps students off the streets until they grow up. School teaches students how to think and socializes them. School teaches the three "R"s: reading, writing, and arithmetic. But difficult students cannot learn the three Rs until they learn the most important, first R: responsibility.

Perhaps the most fundamental and important goal of schooling is teaching the tools of responsible behavior. Virtually every school mission statement includes this concept. Unfortunately, the day-to-day process of discipline in most schools focuses far more on creating obedience. Although obedience is necessary for children to learn, it is in many ways the opposite of responsibility. Obedience requires students to do what they are told. Responsibility requires students to make their own decisions. When people behave responsibly, they make the best decisions they can with their ability and understanding of the consequences.

We all make mistakes and learn from them, and we then go on to make new mistakes. Sometimes we do not learn from our mistakes and go on repeating them until we finally learn our lesson. Unless it has life-threatening consequences, making a mistake is not a tragedy. Not learning from a mistake is. Certainly, obedience is important. Without it, society, schools, and families could not function. We need limits or rules that are followed without choice. But we also need the freedom to make our own decisions. Finding a balance between obedience and responsibility can be difficult. If we require too much obedience, children will not learn how to make decisions on their own or to rebel when they should. Require too little responsibility, however, and a child's life can become unstructured, unpredictable, and chaotic. The balance lies in establishing rules or limits for what is not negotiable, while teaching students to behave responsibly. This balance is the core of an effective discipline plan.

Discipline models that teach responsibility differ most from those that teach obedience in how consequences are chosen and delivered. A model that teaches obedience uses punishments as deterrents, seeks to create the fear of bad consequences when students break the rules, and rewards students for doing what is expected of them. Punishments and rewards may be effective for a limited time in the presence of an authority figure, but they will become almost entirely ineffective in the absence of that authority. Punishments and rewards teach students that breaking the rules is okay as long as they do not get caught and that they should be rewarded for good behavior. The

that pairs new students with "ambassadors" who show them "the ropes," including the school's do's and don'ts. The school discovered that some of its best "ambassadors" were its most difficult students.

Provide healthy, viable choices. Choices are different from limits in that we can expand the number of choices while holding firm on the limits. Choices are often replacements for unacceptable behavior: "You cannot throw your books on the floor, but you can be angry in other ways. You can calm yourself by talking, writing, or coloring." Choices must also be real. A threat presented as a choice is not a real choice because it does not improve a student's ability to make decisions. Instead, it is simply a more sophisticated form of bullying. Telling a student to "either stop interrupting or receive a detention" is a threat. The difference between a threat and a choice is control. When the teacher knows which answer is correct or there is only one way to respond (the teacher's way), then there is no choice, only a threat. By contrast, real choices have at least two alternatives that are acceptable, and a teacher will have no preconceived preference for one or more of the alternatives. If the teacher does have a preference, he or she takes responsibility by sharing it: "I want you in class on time because I miss you when you aren't here and I'd prefer to avoid the hassle of writing a referral." The following examples illustrate the difference between threatening a student and giving him or her a choice.

- Threat: "Stop interrupting or you'll receive a detention."

- Choice: "Stop interrupting. If you really want to tell me something, you can either raise your hand or write it down and meet with me privately when we can discuss your concern without interrupting the class."

The student must see the choices as viable. If we offer a choice a student would never select, then it is not a real choice.

Asking a student to "either tell me which of your friends did it or face the consequence yourself" is a choice most students would never make. Sometimes it is difficult to predict what might be a viable choice for a student, but common sense can help. Students rarely see as viable any choice that they perceive as a violation of their values or culture or of the values or culture of their friends (especially boy- and girlfriends), parents, or other teachers.

Help students learn from consequences. Consequences are the results of our choices. Consequences should be based on rules (limits) and guided by principles (values) that directly relate to and reinforce the reason for the rules. It is much more effective, for example, to ask a student to do something nice for the person he or she has offended (a consequence based on the principle of making amends) than to make the student take a timeout and sit quietly for 10 minutes (a punishment). As long as consequences do not involve danger or other unacceptable outcomes, they are superior to external punishments.

Without consequences, students learn that their choices are irrelevant, that their behavior has no influence on themselves or others. The reality is, however, that our choices always have consequences even though they may be hidden or subtle. However, some natural consequences may not be effective deterrents in a school setting. For example, one consequence for hitting another student is that the student might not like the attacker any longer. That consequence will probably do little to prevent the misbehaving student from hitting again. Another consequence, such as having the student write a behavior plan or practice appropriate behavior, may teach that hitting is wrong and that there are better ways to express negative feelings.

Elicit commitment to change. Anyone who has tried to lose weight, save money, or become more organized knows how difficult it is to change behavior. We believe that changing our own behavior is the most difficult of life's challenges. If we have trouble changing our own behavior when we want to change, imagine how difficult it is to change a child's behavior when he or she does not want to change. Without a commitment to change from the child, there is little hope that any intervention will have lasting results.

Developing a commitment to change in students is not easy, because it requires that students not only agree that what they did was inappropriate, but also be willing to change even if it requires hard work. We can facilitate commitment to change by:

- remaining connected to the student (especially during incidents of misbehavior),

- sharing our feelings of disappointment in a poor choice,

- expecting that the student will be able to make a better choice, and then

- guiding the student through a problem-solving process that includes practicing a new behavior.

Adding our generous encouragement and support will increase the possibility of long-term change.

Develop remorse. Many educators we have met have commented on the general lack of remorse in today's students. Not only do a significant number of students break rules more regularly, but too many seem not to care or even think that their behavior is unacceptable. When disciplining students, a teacher is as likely to hear "who cares?" as "I'm sorry." This lack of remorse is as serious a problem as the student's misbehavior. Remorse is an essential emotion for long-term behavior change.

Without remorse, students are unlikely to have the will or commitment necessary for the sustained effort to change their behavior whether someone is watching or not.

It is no surprise that feelings of remorse are on the decline. We rarely see public figures show remorse when they are caught or seen doing something wrong. Politicians, ballplayers, members of the clergy, business people, members of the media, physicians, and even educators have all been in the news saying that they are "responsible" for various negative outcomes although they did nothing wrong personally. Increasingly, public figures blame others for their misdeeds. It is the rare public figure who says, "I did it, and I'm truly sorry. I regret it, and I won't do it again." Likewise, some parents blame their children for their parenting mistakes rather than telling the child that they were wrong. Parents who abuse their children never say they beat the child because they are ineffectual adults with arrested character development. They say the child deserved it.

In order for children to learn remorse, they must see others demonstrate it publicly and learn the value of remorse. In addition, remorse must be expected of them. One of the most effective lessons you can give is to show genuine remorse when you make a mistake. Students can see through phony attempts at contrition, just as adults can when they hear public figures say what is right but not mean it.

Teaching remorse is not easy, because it is based on values. Asking students how they feel about what they have done is a first step in getting students to think about what they value and feel remorse. Examples of such questions are:

- "How do you feel, knowing you have hurt Jamie?"

- "How does it feel when someone takes something of yours?"

- "Just about all people feel upset and angry when their stuff is taken. I'll bet you feel that way too, sometimes."

We can follow this line of inquiry with a question that requires the student to think about making amends: "What are you going to do to fix things for Jamie so that she feels better?"

Continually stressing the concept of remorse when involved in discipline situations will have an impact. Having the class develop statements of values to be used for establishing rules can also make a difference. A statement of value would be: "School is a place where we learn that my way is not the only way." A rule developed from this value would be: "Settle disagreements with words, not fists" (Curwin & Mendler, 1997). All disciplinary decisions and discussions could then be based on the values the violator helped to develop. Rules would carry more weight because they would be based on class values. In addition, the violator would be encouraged to feel remorse through consequences when he or she is asked to identify ways to make amends: "How are you going to fix it to make it right?"

Even more influential in the decline of remorse is the increasing use of short-term discipline interventions that provide an easy, "escalator" approach to handling misbehavior. Many educators rely on rewards and punishments for discipline, but these methods do not teach remorse. Instead, they teach students to think of misbehavior as a game. They teach students to make excuses, blame others, hide their misbehavior, or grandstand. Punishments may be effective as a deterrent with "good" students who have already developed the value of caring for others, but they are ineffective with difficult students who have likely received too many punishments from harsh, neglectful, or abusive parents and misguided educators.

Remorse comes from values, and values should be a major part of any model of behavior change. The following methods and practices will help you develop remorse in your students by creating within them the desire to change.

Use welcoming techniques to help the child feel that he or she is part of the group or class. The more the student feels part of the group, the more likely the student will feel remorse for disrupting the group and will want to change from within. Welcoming means more than just greeting. It means letting the student know how glad you are that he or she is part of your group. For example, when a student is removed, you can say that you are sorry he will be gone, that you will miss him, and that you look forward to a better time when he returns. When disciplining a student, you can tell her that you will not give up on her or on trying to find a way to improve your relationship.

Remember that your words mean little if you are not sincere. Be a role model who shows remorse by apologizing and correcting yourself when you have done something you regret, even if it has not hurt someone else. Show genuine remorse when you break a promise, lose your temper, or make a mistake. Being a role model for how to behave in other difficult situations as well is the most effective lesson you can give your students. When a student is disrespectful to you, demonstrate to everyone how to respond to disrespect. If you are called a jerk or worse, respond the same way you want students to respond when they are offended.

Teach rather than tell. Students rarely feel remorse for not doing what they do not know how to do. Yet most of us tell children what to do when they break rules, rather than teaching them what to do differently in the future. We never say "add better" when a student makes a mistake in math. Instead, we teach the student how to understand a problem and solve it correctly. The same approach should be used in interventions. When a student is disrespectful, you might respond by saying, "Next time you are upset, try telling how you feel instead of calling names. It sounds like this: 'I get very upset when you take my things without asking. Please stop doing it.' Why don't you try saying that to me so I can be sure you know how to do it."

Provide support for slippage (regressions). Imagine you have been on a diet for two weeks. In a moment of temptation, you eat an entire chocolate cream pie instead of one small piece. What kind of comment from a friend would help you return to the diet?

"I thought you were on a diet! That's not dieting—that's pigging out. There's no hope for you!"

Or

"Diets are hard sometimes. You had a small backslide and that's normal. Don't give up now. If you go back to what you were doing, this pie won't make any difference. I hope you enjoyed the pie. Maybe in a couple of months you can have another one."

Students need the same encouragement and support when they suddenly slide back into old patterns of behavior. This is a normal part of the process for long-term change. What happens next will determine how successful this process will be. If you respond to a student's slippage with messages of disappointment or failure, the student will most likely give up and believe he or she is incapable of continuing. If you only support without some prodding, the student might falsely think that the goal is not important and that it is okay to give it up. If you respond with understanding, encouragement, and a gentle but firm push to keep trying, the student will most likely see the reversal as temporary and continue to work toward lasting change.

RESPONSIBILITY IS NOT EASY

The first "R" is more difficult to achieve than obedience and often harder to live with when we get it from students. The independent thinking developed by responsibility is more likely to lead to challenges from our students than the compliant behavior developed by obedience. However, most teachers prefer students who challenge classroom ideas related to content over those who simply take notes and regurgitate information on exams. Nevertheless, students who challenge behaviorally do create more discomfort in a classroom. But some of our most gratifying moments as educators will come when we see students monitor themselves, realize that they have choices, show concern for others, and assume responsibility for their behavior at school. The quest for developing student responsibility is a mountain climb, complete with challenge, uncertain footing, occasional obstacles, and the hope of eventual mastery. Patience and a guide to the top are needed to conquer the complexity of the task. The frameworks and strategies in the following chapters provide a guide toward developing student responsibility.

3

Change Starts Within

We cannot expect more of our students than we expect of ourselves. We must act the way we expect our students to behave.

I F WE WANT TO WORK EFFECTIVELY with difficult students, we must be willing to change ourselves. Although we rarely appreciate our most difficult students because of the time they take and the frustration they cause, their presence can lead to professional growth if we learn from the obstacles they throw in our way. Nothing new has been invented by people who are satisfied with the status quo. Dissatisfaction and tension caused by misbehavior can lead us to invent new approaches that could benefit all of our students. In his book, *Don't Sweat the Small Stuff,* Carlson (1997) suggests that instead of asking "Why is he doing this to me?" when someone does something you do not like, ask "What is he trying to teach me?"

Difficult students do not always generate feelings of opportunity. They are frustrating and time consuming, and they interfere with our efforts to teach. Even worse, they make us confront our own difficulty in changing ourselves. As we understand our struggle to change ourselves and find ways to overcome our obstacles, we can better appreciate the difficulties our students face when they try to change. This understanding and appreciation will help us help our students.

Change is perhaps the hardest of all human endeavors. The difficulties faced by people who smoke cigarettes when they decide to quit smoking show how hard it is to change behavior, even when that behavior is self-destructive and the person knows how destructive it is. People who smoke know it is an expensive habit that can have serious health consequences, but they still might try to quit many times and continue to smoke over many years before they finally kick the habit.

In the classroom, educators often find themselves making choices when confronted with difficult students, knowing in advance that what they are doing will not really help or will actually worsen the situation. In our work with educators, we are often asked why it is so hard to change even when we know exactly what to do differently. This chapter examines the influences that can limit our interactions with difficult students and provides ways to overcome them.

WORKING WITHIN LIMITED FRAMEWORKS

Our definition of success determines our choice of interventions. If we define success as silencing a student who calls out, we will behave differently than if we define success as ensuring that the student no longer wants to call out at inappropriate times. By changing our frameworks, we can often find remarkable new solutions.

Strategies for improvement. I once told a friend that I was a terrible speller. He disagreed while offering a unique perspective: "You just haven't learned to spell every word yet. Think of all the words that you can spell perfectly!" The same framework applies to how we perceive difficult students. They make some good decisions, but they have not learned to make every decision a good one. They make a lot of bad decisions and have not yet learned how to make better ones or do not yet understand how a different decision will actually give them more hope.

Developing discipline goals within this framework enables us to evaluate our interventions by how well they instruct rather than by how well they ensure short-term compliance. Much of this work involves reframing, one of the most important strategies we can use when we work with challenging students. How you "label" these students often defines how they will behave. Do your labels support and affirm the students or do they demonize and accuse? Try changing labels like "lazy" to "has yet to find value in the lessons" or "defiant" to "sticks up for himself." We can often reframe by giving credit to the motive or goal of the student behavior while disagreeing with the method: "I see that you have many important priorities. Let's find a way to make your studies one of them."

Examples. Billy grabs Andy's pencil. Frame it this way: Billy has not found an acceptable way to seek attention, get a pencil, or express his anger. Determine or guess his need, and teach him how to meet it without grabbing.

Makeesha comes late to class and is often unprepared. Frame it this way: Makeesha cares enough to show up. Can you genuinely and prominently affirm her for coming while encouraging her to come more often and providing consequences for her lack of preparation?

OFFERING A LIMITED SELECTION OF CHOICES

Sometimes we know the goal, but do not know how to achieve it. Our choices of intervention do not include any that will help us reach our most important goals. If our goal is to create an active learning environment, but using threats is the only technique we know, we will not be able to achieve our goal until we learn new techniques.

Strategies for improvement. Describe your goal for your classroom on a sheet of paper. Then evaluate your intervention strategies by listing them on another sheet (or sheets) of paper and putting a checkmark by those that hinder your goal. What is left? If nothing is left, imagine you are a student in your classroom, and ask yourself what would help you learn. You can also ask difficult students what they think would be most helpful for them to learn better behavior.

Example. Esam throws rocks on the playground. Removing him will not work because he cannot improve his playground behavior without being on the playground. Scolding him seems to make him sneakier, and he will not listen to reason. What is left? You are at a loss. Can you think of what would help you if you were Esam? Meet with him to discuss how he needs to learn a different way of expressing himself on the playground and ask him to identify what would help him change his behavior. You might even suggest that Esam think of ways to fix the problem (e.g., clean up the playground) or otherwise make restitution.

FEELING PRESSURED TO "DO SOMETHING"

A classroom discipline situation creates pressure for an immediate solution. The result may be an instinctive desire to act before we are ready to choose the best action. We may feel compelled to show our authority to other students, parents, or colleagues. We may believe that we just cannot let the kid "get away with it." A teacher who does not want to appear mean might not draw a clear enough limit, while another who wants praise in the faculty room for "not letting them get away with things" might be too harsh. Whatever the reason, we feel pressured to "do something now!" Think about what could happen in other professions if people acted on this impulse. What if doctors performed unnecessary surgeries just because they felt they had to do something?

Strategies for improvement. Keep a log of strategies you have tried with challenging students and note how effective they are. If a strategy is ineffective after five trials, stop using it with that student or in that situation. Try at least one new strategy every month to expand your range of choices. Make a personal list of things you have promised never to do again and keep it in sight on your desk. You might also find ways to effectively "buy time" while you are thinking of other options. When you are angry, resist the impulse to react without thought. When students pressure you to know how you plan to react, refuse to gossip about the situation or engage in speculation.

Example. If the inappropriate behavior is very public, you might say, "Probably, most of you are wondering what I'll be doing about this situation. After I've thought it over, I'll let [the misbehaving student] know."

LOSING CONTROL OF OUR EMOTIONS

Because student misbehavior can push our buttons and create a fight-or-flight response within us, it is very important for us to find ways of staying personal with the student without taking the misbehavior personally. When our emotions are stronger than our reason, we will defend ourselves rather than do what is best for the student.

Strategies for improvement. Occasional emotional outbursts might be helpful when they show our students that we are humans with real feelings. However, the classroom is not designed to meet our personal or professional therapy needs. We are responsible for establishing and maintaining a climate for learning. If we are constantly in power struggles with students and continually take students' behavior personally, then we need to take a step back from the situation and try to figure out what is going on. Do we feel this way about many students or just one in particular? Feeling this way about many of our students is often a symptom of high stress, maybe even burnout. In these cases, the best solution may be counseling; a change in assignment, grade level, or subject; or a leave of absence. If we feel this way about only one or two of our students, we need to discover why these students have the ability to push our buttons so frequently. Is there something about the student that makes us angrier than other students make us? Are her words more personal and hurtful? Does he invoke feelings of failure within us? Does she remind us of our own children or of ourselves?

Answering these questions can give us the understanding we need to redefine our relationship with the student or students who push our buttons. Having a frank talk with the student can also help. In private, you could let the student know that she provokes you and that you want to find a way for each of you to provoke each other less. You might work out private signals that warn each other of an impending emotional response that requires the other to back off or approach in a different manner.

Example. You and Connie have a frank discussion about your relationship. You explain that her language makes it hard for you to understand what she is trying to say. She reveals that she uses that language when she feels frustrated because that seems to be the only way anyone listens to her. She agrees on a one-word signal she can use when she thinks you are not listening, giving you the opportunity to assure her that you will listen. You agree on a one-word signal that tells her you are ready to react emotionally, giving her the opportunity to stop using offensive language before you react.

NOT RECOGNIZING STRESS

The loss of emotional control is often one indication of stress. This encompasses more than just anger. If we find that we are often overcome with emotions when teaching, especially frustration, failure, cynicism, or weariness, our stress levels are too high. Stress alters our ability to make good choices. When we are unaware of our level of stress and of our ability to handle it, we cannot monitor or control the effect stress has on us.

Strategies for improvement. There are many ways of keeping stress levels in check (Curwin & Mendler, 1988, 1997). Perhaps the most practical avenue for support at school is to network with other staff who will listen, offer a suggestion, or even keep one of your disruptive students for a brief interval.

Example. Mr. Grant is a high school chemistry teacher with too many students and not enough equipment. He believes the only way to control his overcrowded class is to constantly yell when he needs the students' attention. Neither he nor his students enjoy coming to class. Although he does not like to yell so often, he believes he has no other choice because he has little control over the budget and no control over his class size. As long as he feels helpless, he is unable to find possible solutions. He shares his frustration with his principal, who suggests Mr. Grant organize his classes into groups and give a student in each group, on a rotating basis, responsibility for quieting his or her group when Mr. Grant gives a signal. Mr. Grant tries the strategy and discovers he no longer has to yell, and both he and his students enjoy class more. More importantly, learning increases significantly.

BEING PRESSURED BY OUTSIDE FORCES AND COMMUNITY DEMANDS

The stress we feel as educators does not always come from within our classrooms or even our schools. Sometimes we allow outside forces and community pressures to increase our stress levels and to limit our ability to find effective solutions. While more resources, greater administration approval, smaller classes, more time, and fewer responsibilities would definitely make teaching and disciplining easier, we usually have to live with a significantly different picture.

Strategies for improvement. We may feel helpless when we consider how little influence we have with children compared to the influence of the media and their friends and parents. We may also become frustrated when we think of what we are asked to do and the resources we are given to do it. One of the important lessons we teach children is that they may not be able to control or influence what others do, but they are responsible for how they *respond* to what others do. The same principle holds true for educators. We may not be able to control how students, parents, or colleagues behave, but we can control how we respond. Our position as teaching professionals also gives us the opportunity to occasionally influence what we cannot control. All of our actions should be guided by our goal of helping students be successful and responsible. When challenged by outside pressures, we need to be open to different ways of achieving our goal even as we remain firm in our insistence on the outcome.

Example. A parent complains that you have been treating her child unfairly. Rather than becoming defensive, you can thank the parent for caring enough to share her concern and let her know that you did what you did to help her child become more successful and responsible. If she wants to know why you did not do the exact same thing to another child, you can respond by telling her that while you will not discuss specifics about one child and family with another, you often do different things because different children sometimes need different ways to become *successful* and *responsible*. You can show your openness to the possibility that other interventions might work better by inviting the parent to offer suggestions of successful strategies she has used at home to help her child become more responsible.

GIVING IN TO HABIT

Breaking habits is hard, especially in the pressure of the classroom. Children's behavior often triggers patterned responses in their teachers that are comfortable because of their familiarity. Things that are habitual are easy and convenient for us to do. The longer we have used habitual behavior, the more difficult it is to change. Our past experiences often become equations in our mind, which include a predetermined response. For example, students who call us names become equivalent to disrespect, which requires class removal. We can increase our effectiveness when we let each experience unfold without an internal recording telling us what to do.

Strategies for improvement. Breaking habits is hard work. We can be more successful when we replace a habit rather than break it. Habits lead to linear thinking. When we think linearly, we are rehearsing and choosing our responses before we have finished listening to the student or examining what has occurred. It can be helpful to avoid thinking of our response before we see and hear all of the facts. It can also be helpful to reframe the incident before determining our response.

Example. Instead of yelling for the class to quiet down, tell them softly. Practice this at home, and use the new behavior whether it is needed or not within the first five minutes of class. Ask your students to point out when you revert to the old habit or use audio- or videotape as feedback.

BEING INFLUENCED BY FORMER TEACHERS

Much of our teaching style was developed by watching others teach. Most educators have spent their entire pre-professional lives in the classroom as students and student teachers. We have watched enough teachers in action to form a model of what we think good teachers do in various situations. Our role models exert more influence on our decision making than most of us realize. Although modeling effective teachers is a good way to improve our teaching, another teacher's style may be a bad fit for us. For example, we may have seen sarcasm used effectively by a few rare teachers who can do it in an endearing way. Typically, however, the use of sarcasm alienates students.

Strategies for improvement. Think of the best teachers you have observed through the years, the ones you wanted to be like. How much of the way you interact with children did you incorporate from them? If you can recall, make a list of these teachers and the ways you interact with children. How effective are the strategies for you? Do they give you the results you want? If not, they may not be a good fit for you. They might not have even worked for your role model. Then list the things that you see or hear successful colleagues do (those who are highly respected and liked by faculty and students). After reflecting on the list, pick one or two behaviors that you would like to try. After practicing in the car or in front of a mirror, try the behavior five times with your students to determine if the behavior works for you.

Example. When you make a list of your best teachers and the strategies you learned from them, you include Mrs. Hudson, whose sense of humor you greatly admired. She playfully teased her students, and even though she could be sarcastic when a student misbehaved, her students were never really offended because they knew she cared and enjoyed her sense of humor. You have tried to be funny like Mrs. Hudson, but your students usually respond negatively. After you realize that very few teachers have the knack for making sarcasm funny and personally inoffensive, you give up trying to be like Mrs. Hudson and use strategies that build on your strengths in listening and reflecting when students misbehave.

OVERCOMING THE DIFFICULTY OF CHANGE

There are several helpful approaches and mindsets that are useful in overcoming the difficulty of change.

Reduce isolation. Few people in other professions must perform under the same levels of stress and isolation experienced by teachers. The remedy is to reduce the time we work alone and to increase our opportunities for genuine professional dialogue. Wise administrators:

- Encourage and allow classroom visitations that cross grade and subject lines. Teachers should be seen by and should observe other teachers at least once a month.

- Use faculty meeting time to discuss issues related to student behavior. We prefer to refer to students anonymously for this exercise. Brainstorm lists of methods and techniques that others have successfully used to handle student misbehavior.

- Encourage and support visits to other schools in the district and beyond. During faculty meetings, teachers can report on what they have observed at other schools.

- Find ways to send teachers to professional meetings, association gatherings, conferences, and professional seminars.

Look for common ground. When students make us angry, it becomes easier to demonize them. Demonization is the process of labeling and defining a person or group by their most hated characteristics. When we demonize difficult students, we see them as very different from ourselves. The more we recognize the similarities we share with our most troubling students, the more likely we are to use interventions that are not personally motivated. To look for common ground with one of your difficult students, ask yourself:

- What do I have in common with this student?

- Have I ever broken a similar rule or become angry with a teacher in the same way this student has with me?

- Imagine yourself as the student, using all you know about him or her. Picture yourself in a mental movie, in which you assume the role of the student and the student assumes your role.

Do any of these techniques help you see your troubling students in more human terms? If they do, use them. If they do not, continue searching for common ground until you find it. When you can identify with your most difficult students, you can relate to them in conversation and during behavioral interventions in more understanding, empathetic terms.

Learn from techniques that fail. Another way to work toward positive change is to examine how you respond to a failed technique or to a student who does not respond the way you want. When techniques fail, are you more likely to blame the student, the technique, the parents, the system, or yourself? In general, the desire to place blame is a strong but unhelpful emotion. Instead of trying to place blame or find fault, analyze the technique in relation to the student, the student's needs, or the misbehavior. Try to determine why there was a mismatch and what could be done differently next time.

When we realize how difficult it is to change as adults, we will have more sympathy for our students in their struggles to change. Changing ourselves first can remove many of the barriers between us and our most difficult students, showing them how the change process works. It can also reduce our stress levels and help us more effectively reach and teach all of our students.

Attitudes and Beliefs

Our best students reinforce our belief that what we do works. Our worst students challenge us to grow. We need both.

IMAGINE YOU ARE IN THE CLASSROOM and you ask Anwar a question related to the lesson. Anwar smirks and says, "Who the hell cares—this class sucks!" Li, who cannot concentrate for more than three minutes, decides to take a stroll in the middle of your class. His cruise around the room includes visits with others while you are trying to teach. Shelby is polite and friendly, and even participates in the class lesson occasionally. Unfortunately, she never brings her materials, is usually late, and does not do her homework. José has an extremely short fuse. You just never really know how he will react. There are hours and even days in which he is calm and focused. Then, with no warning at all, he may suddenly go over the top and throw a chair or challenge someone to fight.

Working with difficult students requires instructional and emotional preparation to meet the many challenges they present. As we have noted, there is no simple formula that can be applied in all instances. Nevertheless, certain beliefs and attitudes form the basis of methods and strategies that can help you provide difficult students with a quality education while maintaining your sanity.

BELIEVE THAT CHANGE IS POSSIBLE

Educators must have an unflagging belief in the capacity of human beings to change. We must express or reclaim our sense of optimism if we are to effectively coach our students toward change. It can be very difficult to remain optimistic with our difficult students because they do not change easily or with appreciation. It is easy to give up on them because they burn us out. But unless we awaken our enthusiasm, we will not be able to influence change. Children will not change when they sense or believe that those trying to help them change do not really care.

A refuse-to-give-up, courageous, stay-involved attitude was articulated recently by our friend and colleague Marvin Harrison, as he commented on what it feels like to walk through the halls and see a distressed student: "The temptation is to walk right past and tell myself not to get involved. After all, I am a teacher, an expert in my subject field, not in human behavior. I am also afraid. I don't tell this to anybody, but it is very real to me. Is this kid armed? Will he go off on me? Will I be another good Samaritan who ends up injured? As I look more closely into his eyes, I see his pain. He looks as though he has been so beaten down by life that there is not much life left. His pride is long gone. He does not have a shred of dignity left . . . I step into his world."

STAY PERSONALLY CONNECTED WITHOUT TAKING OFFENSIVE BEHAVIOR PERSONALLY

Sometimes student misbehavior seems to be directed at us, and sometimes it is. But being a professional educator requires us to stay personally involved with each student without taking obnoxious, irritating, disruptive, and hurtful behavior personally. When we personalize an event, we are unlikely to make the best professional choice, and we are rarely able to do what is best for the student.

Approximately 70% of all school misbehavior may have its roots in the home, not school (Curwin, 1990). It is common for student anger to develop at home or on the streets and then be directed at an educator, who is generally a safer target. Like an infant whose cries of hunger are ignored or punished, the intensity of the need only increases when it is not met. These students cannot be reached unless the educator learns how to keep caring in spite of a sometimes overwhelming desire to give up.

When student behavior makes us want to fight back, we face the difficult challenge of finding ways of staying personally involved with the student. Students who attack are virtually always under attack. Fearful of real or imagined harm, they often strike first. If attacked back, a never-ending cycle of aggression can begin. Since these students see the world as a hostile place, they often set others up to reject them so that their worldview is confirmed. Adults and peers must understand and know how to handle this hostility cycle (Curwin & Mendler, 1997) or the conflict cycle (Long & Morse, 1996). Difficult youth who succeed are surrounded by supportive adults and peers who find ways of communicating that the person, and who he or she is, is more important than any misbehavior.

However, caution is necessary when separating how one views a person's behavior from how one views the person as a whole. Some people define themselves by their behavior. For example, "I take drugs because I am an addict. I lie because addicts lie." Further, if enough behavior is unacceptable to you, then you are essentially finding the individual to be unacceptable (i.e., "I like you, but I don't like your language, hygiene, habits, lies, stealing, lack of responsibility. But I like you."). When we continue to care and refuse to give up, these students will often push harder and harder until they finally surrender to the possibility of bonding and change.

A nurse does not yell at a patient who lies bleeding on a gurney, "You can't have surgery until you clean up your mess!" Sometimes students bleed emotionally on us. Like nurses, it is our job to help, not retaliate. Although interventions and consequences are often necessary when students say and do hurtful things, it helps to remember that whatever students dish out to us reflects what they are dealing with on a more regular basis with their significant others. A home visit can give us the perspective we need to put aside our personal needs and remain professional, although we advise that you do not make home visits alone.

CHANGE THE LABEL

An early adolescent, Ned was a challenging, foulmouthed, and aggressive student who frequently created disruptions in his classes. Understandably, his teachers often became frustrated and kicked him out of class. Either the same day or the next, Ned would return with revenge in mind. Power struggles were a regular event. Most everyone kept hoping for an occasional absence, but Ned had perfect attendance. When the staff met to discuss how to handle this situation, we realized that all of his teachers were both frustrated and angry with Ned because of his excessive needs and frequent classroom disruption.

We established a plan that defined the logistics of where Ned would be sent if his behavior became unmanageable. That was the easy part. Much more difficult was figuring out how to keep caring for Ned while preserving the integrity of the class. The first step was to re-label Ned as a "student who felt hurt" rather than a "disruptive rebel." While we did not know exactly who was abusing Ned, it was clear that he had to have been victimized by an important other to be so disrespectful and angry. His teachers were helped to see that when he called them SOBs, they did not *have to* become offended at his offensive behavior. If they chose, they could attribute his offensive behavior to an expression of pain in his own life rather than a personal statement directed at them.

It is possible not to become offended, but it does require work. For example, imagine that if instead of Ned calling his teachers SOBs, he called them a chair, a chalkboard, or an eraser. Immediately, there would be a different reaction. Concern could replace conflict. Instead of "What did you say!" or "Out!" the message might become "I think you're wrong, and I am concerned." We will need to continue providing consequences most of the time, but we can do so in a way that *teaches* the child rather than reinforces the child's belief that "all adults are mean and hurtful."

Shortly after our "brainstorming" conference, one of Ned's teachers was verbally assaulted by him. Upon being referred to as the waste product that comes out of a horse's rear end, she reminded herself to hear the words "chalkboard" and "eraser." She reported that she began laughing at the incongruence between his words and her thoughts. After *choosing* to hear his words in neutral tones, she was able to defuse the moment by saying, "Ned, using those words in front of everyone is upsetting and embarrassing. Neither of us deserves to be embarrassed. If you have anger to share, I promise to hear you after class." She then went on with the class. Later, she dealt privately with him in a manner that enabled her to actually identify some of his anger, which led to a changed relationship. Teachers can give an extremely powerful lesson when they effectively handle an attacking student while showing everyone that dignity can be maintained.

CONTINUE ACCEPTING THE STUDENT WHEN HE OR SHE REJECTS YOU

Part of an unflagging belief in the capacity of challenging students to change is a commitment to being better at accepting these students than they are at rejecting us. Let the student know that you are at least as stubborn as he or she is with an approach that says, "I know the game. You want to do everything you can to push me away, because then you'll prove yet again that everybody and everything is unfair. But I am not going away. I know you've got worth even though you don't think so."

BE AS TOUGH AS NECESSARY

In *Discipline with Dignity* (Curwin & Mendler, 1988) and *As Tough As Necessary: A Discipline with Dignity Approach to Countering Aggression, Hostility, and Violence* (Curwin & Mendler, 1997), we proposed the idea that good discipline requires "being fair, not equal." However, many schools and state and local municipalities have mandated "zero-tolerance" policies that do respond "equally" to school violence. These policies were created to support the value of safety for all students and staff while sending a strict message of control to those who would harm others on school grounds. While there is a lack of empirical data on the effectiveness of zero-tolerance policies, most staff, students, and citizens appear to support this approach. The fear provoked by school shootings and other "out-of-control" behavior has everyone seeking to do something.

Zero tolerance is compatible with the social trend of having less understanding, support, and sympathy for the "criminal" and placing more emphasis on the rights of the victim. Although the desire to empower potential victims is entirely understandable and popular, zero tolerance is an educationally unsound philosophy because it ignores the importance and uniqueness of education and educators. When we carry the zero-tolerance philosophy into our personal lives, it is easy to see how the idea offends our values as educators and responsible adults. No one wants a zero-tolerant spouse, supervisor, or friend. Do we really want to teach our children to have zero tolerance for others?

Like all responsible and concerned educators, we want our schools to be safe. A values-based curriculum like the one described in *As Tough as Necessary* (Curwin & Mendler, 1997) sets the right tone. We feel strongly that most situations in which students harm others or carry weapons warrant strong, clear, immediate, and visible action. There are even times when students must be temporarily or permanently separated from a school that lacks sufficient resources to address their needs. But educators must maintain the essence of who they are and what they do by being "as tough as necessary" rather than "zero tolerant."

For example, most would agree that schools need to do much more to address issues like bullying and sexual harassment. In fact, a survey of teenagers (*USA Weekend*, 1996) found that 33% of boys and 37% of girls in grades 6 through 12 have been "touched, grabbed, or pinched" at school. Few would argue against the need for firm, clear rules and consequences to curtail these problems. But applying the zero-tolerance philosophy to sexual harassment and many other problems locks us into doing things that are at best publicly silly and at worst harmful. How does society or a six-year-old boy benefit when he is suspended from school because he violated the school's policy on sexual harassment by hugging and kissing the cheek of a friend of the opposite sex?

When a fearful, 14-year-old student with a clean record is being intimidated by a street gang and is expelled for bringing a butter knife to school, it is time to move beyond the simplicity of zero tolerance. When school districts and teachers' unions create policies that limit professionals to having only verbal contact (no touching) with students, especially early elementary students, the needs of most young students are denied because of the unfortunate few incidents of abuse or false accusation that make the headlines.

We believe that a school's policy should reflect the diversity of its students and communities. This should include, but not limit itself to, methods of "toughness." Difficult students cannot generally be leveraged into behaving through discipline methods that make them miserable, because they are rarely connected enough with school to feel bothered by the privileges they lose or the scorn they invite. Our methods include being "as tough as necessary" to fit the situation, the students, and our educational values.

BE CREATIVE: INVENT INTERVENTIONS THAT WORK

We recently met a preschool teacher who told us about a four-year-old child who constantly used make-believe guns in his play. He drew guns, built guns with LEGO® blocks, and talked about guns. The teacher's efforts to prohibit such play were met with even more intense, aggressive play. She was trying to promote an atmosphere of cooperation and nonviolence, and was understandably concerned that other children would become aggressive.

When asked if she knew much about this child's background with guns, she dejectedly said that he had seen his cousin killed and that he had been at home in the next room when his uncle was killed in a recent drive-by shooting. Clearly, this young child was stressed, frightened, and preoccupied with these events, and was reliving some or all of this stress through his play. In effect, he had no other place to turn for safety and meaning than to his play.

We helped the teacher realize that she needed to give this child a sense of control and to find alternative ways of meeting his need for guns within his play. She was encouraged to do a lot of active listening by following the themes that he used. The child needed to be engaged by someone who cared and was able to decode the messages for help he was sending. He also needed to know that she would do everything she could to make sure he felt safe in the classroom. He eventually became less obsessed with guns while under the teacher's care. The absence of a strong emotional support network of his own, however, made his long-term outcome far from certain.

Difficult students who do not respond to our "tried and true" strategies give us an opportunity to grow by making us look for and use new strategies. This teacher's usual strategy of prohibiting the student's gun play only intensified the problem. Using the new strategy of actively listening to his play gave the teacher a way to begin to help the boy.

In one way, we gain a considerable amount of freedom by working with challenging youth because, each time they fail to respond to our familiar strategies, we must move beyond the boundaries of what has worked into the frontier of what might work. What is the worst that can happen in uncharted territory? We may find another method that does not work. But in the process, we may discover something that does work. When we understand how our most difficult students may be our most valuable lessons in teaching, we can be grateful to them for helping us expand our limits and find strategies that help all students.

One thing to keep in mind as you work with difficult youth is that not all students have deep-seated, intractable problems. Sometimes, all you need to do is look beyond your routine responses for a simple, creative solution. A high school teacher in Lawrence, New Jersey, recently shared with us a method he discovered out of exasperation with an attention-seeking student who often interrupted the lesson. After trying most conventional methods, he said, "Bob, I don't know why you are constantly seeking attention in this class, but I think out of respect we ought to give you all the attention you want. So from this point on, I'll notice you at all times, we'll stop the class for as long as necessary and give you the attention you need." After the third day of being in the spotlight, Bob had had enough. He was fine thereafter.

EXPECT TO FEEL UNEASY AS YOU TRY NEW THINGS

Noted educator and author Madeline Hunter was quoted as saying, "If you want to feel secure, do what you already know how to do. If you want to be a true professional and continue to grow . . . go to the cutting edge of your competence, which means a temporary loss of security. So, whenever you don't quite know what you're doing, know you're growing." Difficult students give us many unexpected opportunities to demonstrate such professionalism and growth. Because the results of our efforts are usually neither immediate nor permanent, persistence is necessary. Our guideline is that any discipline method that makes sense is worth trying at least five times or implementing for a minimum of two weeks. If there is no evidence the method leads to better behavior after five tries or two weeks, then it is usually time to move on and try something else.

STUDENTS BECOME MORE RESPONSIBLE WHEN THEY ARE GIVEN THE OPPORTUNITY TO BE RESPONSIBLE

What would we think of a coach who said, "Eric, in the last game you missed most of your free throws. You will not be permitted to practice shooting foul shots until you improve"? Or a reading teacher who said, "Clarissa, you do not read up to grade level. You cannot read a single book until your scores are raised"? How different are these cases from telling a student who misbehaves on the playground to report to in-school detention with no more playground privileges? Or removing a student from a field trip for proving he does not possess "field-trip skills"? Students cannot learn responsible behavior when they are removed from the very environment that teaches it. It is preferable to keep the student in the environment while simultaneously teaching the skills needed for success. If more resources are needed for teaching, then they must be secured or the student should be placed in an environment that can provide the kind of teaching opportunities he or she needs. Of course, careful monitoring of the student might be wise, especially if the student is on a field trip where safety is an issue. A parent assigned to stay close to the student will help a great deal.

GUARD AGAINST BURNOUT

Today's society rarely shows its appreciation for or validates our efforts to improve the lives of challenging youth. Far too many people think educators work too little, make too much money, and achieve mediocre results. As we know, however, a successful educator is a teacher, social worker, nurse, friend, police officer, and parent. Continually working with difficult students can be extremely stressful. Unfortunately, such stress sometimes prompts a fight-or-flight response. Neither of these two responses is productive when working with hard-to-reach youth. One leads to power struggles, while the other leads to indifference.

Professional educators can do a number of things to immunize themselves against burnout and to give themselves periodic "booster shots." We need to learn how to stand up for ourselves without fighting back. We need to let the student know that his or her behavior is unacceptable in a way that moves beyond our own rage at what feels like a personal attack or failure. We must find ways to preserve our dignity and leadership in the classroom even as we protect the dignity of the troubled student. Difficult students are masterful at knowing how to make us angry and upset. One way to stand up for yourself when you are angered is to use "I" messages and invite the student to communicate with different words. When you do so in an assertive, respectful tone, this strategy is a relatively safe way to convey upset, frustrated feelings. For example: "I am disappointed in your choice of language. Most students who use those kind of words are trying to say they are either hurt or angry. I am concerned about you and look forward to seeing you after class. I want to hear your side of the story."

To be mentally prepared to handle challenging behavior, we must take good emotional care of ourselves. We know that students need nonviolent ways of responding to provocation. Educators do, too. We need to learn and practice relaxation strategies that can help calm us down when our buttons are pushed. Basic relaxation techniques include counting to ten, visualizing a peaceful scene, and/or doing deep breathing before you respond. Although each of us has a preferred method of relaxing when the situation around us becomes increasingly stressful, we often fail to use it. The key to relaxation strategies is not so much finding the one that works as using it when it matters most.

At school, taking periodic timeouts from difficult students may provide temporary relief. Educators can make prior arrangements to help each other when they need a break from a frustrating student. We recently visited a middle school that has a "pink envelope" system. Any teacher who sends a student to the office with a pink envelope is requesting a 15-minute respite from that student. Similar arrangements can be made with fellow teachers when necessary.

Managing our own stress effectively enables us to mentor students who need us the most, and healthy adult mentoring is one of the most important factors in helping at-risk youth make better choices. The trust and common bond provided by a mentoring relationship enable challenging youth to leave the safety of their self-defeating thoughts and behaviors. We must move beyond our natural, counterproductive responses to stress and respond in ways that further our bonding with and caring for difficult youth.

In summary, skills for changing student behavior flow from attitudes of caring, trusting, risking, and reaching out in ways beyond what our emotions dictate. We believe these attitudes define a professional educator. Professionals understand that discipline is an integral part of their job. They understand that discipline takes time to plan, patience to implement, and a refusal to give up despite the rejection and defiance shown by so many challenging students.

5

Why Students Misbehave

When told to sit down or else, the student said, "I'll sit down, but in my mind, I'm still standing."

STUDENT BEHAVIOR IS NOT RANDOM. When students make poor choices from our perspective, they are making the best choices from theirs. Student misbehavior is often an inappropriate attempt to meet very appropriate needs. When we understand why students misbehave and respond directly to their *needs*, we have a much better chance of helping them change than when we simply respond to their *behavior*. For example, two students showing the same behavior may be trying to meet two very different needs. Robert throws his books on the floor because he has finished his work and is bored. Juana throws her books on the floor because she cannot do the work and has not even begun it. Although both students acted out in the same way, their different needs would not be met if the same behavioral intervention was used with both of them.

An effective intervention responds directly to the motive behind the problem behavior and decreases the likelihood of further misbehavior. Responses that only focus on the incident are insufficient in the same way that some medicines stop the pain but do nothing to cure the disease. Behavioral psychology and reinforcement theory in particular have been woefully inadequate in providing educators with practical and effective means of intervention. Conventional reinforcement theory suggests that "ignoring" the behavior will eventually eliminate it. If the student is seeking only the teacher's attention, then ignoring might be a possible intervention. But if attention from classmates is sought, then ignoring student behavior will not adequately address the problem. In fact, ignoring demands for attention is rarely, if ever, useful. Students who need attention either scream louder or act out in more dramatic ways. Ignoring Juana, for example, does not address her concern if she is acting out because she is worried about her competence (i.e., she is afraid of looking stupid so she tries to hide behind misbehavior).

In the past, researchers have used a basic needs framework to explain problem behavior and identify successful practices in handling misbehavior (Brendtro, Brokenleg, & Van Bockern, 1990; Dreikurs, 1964; Glasser, 1986; Maslow, 1968; Mendler, 1992; Sagor, 1996). Our observations and research suggest that these basic needs are:

- belonging
- attention
- competence/mastery
- power/influence

- empathy

- fun/stimulation and

- relevance

Discipline problems occur when students either come to school with unmet basic needs or the school fails to address a basic need. It is in every educator's professional self-interest to understand how unmet basic needs can lead to problem behavior and to implement classroom practices that address each of these needs. When these basic needs are met, students are much calmer and more interested, motivated, and enthusiastic at school.

We need to look more deeply into the motives behind student misbehavior and the unmet psychological needs behind those motives so that we can understand, diagnose, and respond to our students more effectively. Just as proper treatment of a medical ailment depends on an accurate diagnosis, influencing a student's behavior depends on identifying what he or she needs—the kind of diagnosis any classroom teacher can learn to make. We are not suggesting that teachers become psychologists. Nevertheless, the more attuned we are to psychodynamic motives and needs, the better able we are to create effective short-term and long-term strategies.

MAKING THE DIAGNOSIS: DISCOVERING WHY STUDENTS MISBEHAVE

Some teachers reject the idea that diagnosing their students' needs is part of teaching, mostly because they are afraid they have neither the training nor the skills to do so. Fortunately, it does not take a trained therapist to master the diagnostic process. Good parents do it all the time with no training at all. Do not be afraid of making mistakes. Most doctors make a diagnosis through the process of elimination, as they rule out possible explanations when treatment does not work. Diagnosing the wrong need will do no harm. If things do not improve when you act on your diagnosis, simply cross that need off the list and try again. It is helpful to remember that needs are often interwoven. Meeting one need often helps you meet others.

1) THEY WANT TO BE NOTICED AND FEEL CONNECTED

Consider the behavior of Germaine, a 16-year-old, impulsive, and occasionally aggressive ninth-grader, who disrupts his math class about every two minutes. He is asthmatic and wheezes, and he occasionally falls asleep in class and snores. We do not know how, or whether, his medical condition influences his behavior. It is not unusual for him to take a mid-class stroll through the room as he playfully disturbs classmates. When asked why he disrupts class, he claims not to know or he quickly states that he loves attention and likes to act like a baby. When asked how he wants to be remembered by classmates, he says, "funny." He is polite to his teacher when she corrects him, but the improved behavior lasts for only a moment or two.

A number of unmet basic needs are at the root of Germaine's disruptive behavior. Germaine's primary need is to be noticed and feel connected. He wants attention from his classmates. Students who misbehave for attention will usually do numerous minor, irritating things. They may drop a pencil frequently with an "on-purpose" grin. They may call out answers without thinking, make noises, or burp. They often have perfect attendance. A 1984 cartoon by Mike Streff shows a child in the kitchen with his mother and illustrates one teacher's exasperated response to this need for attention. The child looks up at his mother and says, "My teacher wants a written excuse for my presence." The expression of this need for attention is increasing in schools as the amount of attention received at home from family members decreases for many children.

Challenge: Identify classroom practices that give students a feeling of belonging. Most people feel they belong when they feel welcome and important. What are some things you might say and do that would give more special attention to those who seem to need it?

⟩ THEY WANT TO HIDE FEELINGS OF INADEQUACY

Most people think it is better to be thought of as bad than as stupid. In our culture, if you are good at being bad, then you are in the running for a TV movie. If you are very good at being bad, then you might even make it to the big screen. Those who become notorious like Jesse James are part of American folklore. Rarely do we celebrate the lives of those who are limited or "stupid" unless they turn out to be smarter than we are. Students who worry about looking stupid will either withdraw and become "unmotivated" or act out when they should be working. These students generate in teachers the feeling that "if only you tried harder, you would do better," yet they seem to be satisfied with underachieving. Those who act out will often be friendly and even well-behaved during the times they are not asked to perform. But when called on, given a test, or in some other way required to show their mastery, these students will act out verbally or protest by action (i.e., dropping a pencil) or inaction.

Challenge: Students hiding feelings of stupidity usually have major issues around their basic need for competence/mastery. They need to believe that they can and will succeed when they make an effort. These students usually need to feel appreciated for their efforts and for what they have already accomplished rather than feeling that they always have to do more in order to be successful. We need to let them know that we believe they are capable when they try. Emphasize their accomplishments, even when minimal, as a way to encourage more effort ("You got answers 1, 3, and 6 right. Looks like you are on your way. Congratulations."). These students need to know that their effort is at least as important as their achievement.

3) THEY DO NOT KNOW BETTER

It is no longer sensible to assume that students know how they are supposed to act but are just being obstinate when they misbehave. Teachers should always assume that appropriate standards of behavior need to be taught, not simply announced. When lack of knowledge is the underlying cause of misbehavior, students will show improvement when they know what is expected, have had opportunities to practice the desired behavior, and understand the connection between the rules and the reasons for the rules. Some students may know the expectations, but do not understand what purpose they serve or on what values they are based. For example, they may "know" that wearing a hat is unacceptable, but they do not understand how wearing a hat can affect learning. Let these students know how the rules promote and safeguard learning. Demonstrate how the value system in a school that promotes courtesy or learning requires that students remove their hats. Other students may know and understand the rules but may be unskilled or lack practice with the required behavior. For example, being tough by adopting a swaggering gait and no-nonsense talk may be required for survival on the street, but this behavior is entirely unacceptable in the classroom.

Challenge: Take a fresh look at your rules and expectations. Be sure that they are clear and specific. Ask yourself, "How do these expectations promote learning?" Answering this question will usually reveal the reasons for the rules. These reasons give the rules their meaning and generally reflect values related to civility (i.e., respect, safety). Be sure that you have fully explained and discussed these reasons with your students. With students who chronically break these rules, have at least five separate sessions to practice the appropriate behavior. These might be held after school, during recess, or at another designated time. During practice sessions, show the student that you understand his or her need by verbally acknowledging it, while emphasizing the idea that there are more appropriate ways to meet it: "I know that you don't usually ask before you borrow, and with some people, that's OK. But in school, it is more helpful to ask. Let's practice." Failure to show progress after several practice sessions would rule out "not knowing better" as the cause of the problem.

4) THEY ARE RULED BY IMPULSE

Some students want to behave better but cannot. They have an acting-out engine that will not stop and only seems to accelerate toward more and more misbehavior. They either cannot find the brakes for their behavior or when they try to use them, nothing much changes. Many of these students have been diagnosed as having Attention Deficit/Hyperactivity Disorder (AD/HD). Others may have the same symptoms but be clinically undiagnosed. Students who "can't" behave can often be identified through their history and efforts. As infants and toddlers, many were "hyperactive" in their sleep. As children, most look puzzled when problem behaviors are brought to their attention. They seem confused by requests for better behavior because they cannot easily understand how their behavior is inappropriate. Often they are unaware of what they are doing and are not lying if they deny it, even though the behavior seems obvious to others.

It is common for these students to try to control their behavior, but success is hard to achieve and often short-lived. Many of these students respond positively to more traditional methods of behavior modification, such as positive reinforcement, because the structure helps them stay organized and focused. In addition, they are often open to learning and practicing methods of self-monitoring and self-control. Their impulse-control problems may make it more difficult to gain a personal sense of competence and mastery. As a result, these students usually welcome skill-based methods that will help them manage their self-control problems. Finally, regular doses of prescription medications designed to counteract AD/HD symptoms usually have a rapid, positive impact on student behavior. Students who do not respond to medication may have been incorrectly diagnosed with AD/HD.

Challenge: For students who act impulsively, clearly define your expectations (preferably in collaboration with them and their parents) and develop organized ways to monitor the students' progress toward meeting these expectations. Using behavior modification and helping these students learn self-monitoring techniques can often provide needed (and appreciated) structure and direction.

5) THEY SEEK FUN AND STIMULATION

In our workshops, we often ask educators to tell us why their students break rules. Invariably, the answers include fun, challenge, and stimulation. We ask educators to remember a time when they had fun breaking a rule. Nearly everyone can. We conclude by asking if they can remember a time when they broke a rule, had fun, were caught, experienced a consequence, and decided that breaking the rule was still worth it. Many have such a memory.

Some people make their living doing dangerous things for stimulation. Police, firefighters, soldiers, race car drivers, and stunt performers come immediately to mind. Many more people join others in raucous activity just for the "fun of it." Some get hooked on their audience's response to their sense of humor so that they constantly tell jokes, make quips, and otherwise practice to become the next Jay Leno.

Students who act out to satisfy their need for fun are usually very likable and engaging. Many teachers note that they would love to have these students in class if they did not have to teach them. These students may improve if you provide classroom entertainment opportunities for them. You can usually negotiate these opportunities. For example, Mrs. DeWitt approaches Paul before class and says, "Paul, you've got a great sense of humor. You lighten up the class, and we need that. However, we also need to cover the lesson. So how many jokes do you think you'll need to tell today?" After Paul offers a number they can agree on, Mrs. DeWitt says, "Will it be best for you to tell them all in a row at the beginning of class; at the end; or a few early, a couple in the middle, and one at the end? I can live with any of these choices." Some teachers report that giving the class "silly" time seems to satisfy their students' need for fun when they are trying to satisfy the need through constant giggling or playing off of one another's misbehavior. The goal is to reduce undesirable behavior by controlling how much is permissible.

Challenge: When students act silly and play off of one another, it may be time to vary the lesson. Consider these behaviors as a cue to change from one style of presentation (lecture) to another (group discussion). Ask the class to help you think of class times when jokes and humor will help learning, such as before or after tests. Set up humor zones for these times. In planning a lesson, identify at least three different ways of presenting the information that you value and then vary your presentation as needed. A good game plan includes the "plays" you think will work as well as backup plays in case they do not.

6) THEY DO NOT SEE THE CONNECTION BETWEEN SCHOOL AND LIFE

Many educators recognize that most of what they teach is soon forgotten. For many students who come to school motivated by strong familial messages on the value and importance of education, the relevance of any class is a secondary issue. They work because they know that they need to do well in school to succeed in life. Without that framework, however, many students see no reason to do things that have no relevance to their lives, like looking at potato or cheek cells under a microscope or learning to identify different types of triangles. The students who complain about being bored, who often appear bored, and who wonder aloud why they have to learn and do things are really questioning relevance. Group misbehavior in which students feed off of one another is another way students question the relevance of what is being taught. When students have increasing expectations for immediate gratification, and sensory stimulation is available and abundant, is it any wonder that they are more likely to misbehave when they do not see how school relates to their lives?

Challenge: Make at least as strong an effort to describe and explain the purpose of the content as you do to teach it. As you read through your curriculum guide, ask yourself the same kinds of challenging and sometimes irritating questions that students ask you: Why do we have to know this? How will knowing this make me a better person? How does this information connect with real-life events? The answer to the last question is especially important for concrete learners. Finally, use specific terms to write down the objectives of each lesson.

When you share these objectives with your students, they know what they will learn and master by the end of a class or a sequence of classes. When there is no immediate or visible relevance to the objectives, it is especially important for motivational purposes to clearly identify and then achieve the day's objectives. For example, when students expect they will know how to identify an isosceles triangle by the end of class, gaining that knowledge can fulfill their need for competence and mastery, even if they have no idea how this knowledge will benefit their lives.

If we cannot connect the content with students, we can often succeed with enthusiasm and our love for the subject. Everyone is attracted to energy and enthusiasm. We pay the most money to watch top athletes, musicians, and performers share their passion and energy with us. You can tap into your own passion and energy by asking yourself what you love about what you teach and then sharing that love with your students. They might not find the content immediately relevant, but they will connect emotionally with your enthusiasm, which will make them want to show up and be with you. The more they are with you, like you, and respect you, the more interested they will become in what interests you. Think of all the courses you had to take and expected to hate, but found yourself loving. Most often, the teacher's energy and enthusiasm won you over. Another suggestion is to do one activity every day in class that you personally love doing. It may be a short, two-minute stunt or take an entire class period. Your students will feel your excitement and become caught up in the contagious energy you create.

7) THEY CANNOT EMPATHIZE

Sadly, too many children have learned to harden their feelings toward others. For protection, abused and neglected children often shut down their ability to care for others because they have discovered early on that caring and pain are synonymous. These children are often in trouble outside of school and known by law enforcement at early ages. They are particularly vulnerable to joining gangs. At school, these children seem to lack a conscience and are oblivious to how their behavior affects others. Even worse, they enjoy giving others pain. If they are to have any hope of becoming sensitive to the needs of others, they need opportunities to help and give (Curwin, 1990).

<u>These children often improve when they realize they have the power to influence other people's lives by doing good deeds.</u> Years ago, we worked with a group of juvenile delinquents who were trained to be clowns. They took their clowning skills to nursing homes and nursery schools to deliver joy to others. This was a transforming experience for many of the boys. For the first time in their lives, they realized they could make a positive difference with others. In a similar manner, successful programs have paired severely disabled children with troubled court-adjudicated youth who are responsible for mentoring and building a relationship with the disabled children.

Challenge: Children who lack conscience show little altruism, empathy, or generosity to others. They can be frightening. It takes courage for educators to engage these youngsters because giving up can feel like welcome relief. The main challenge is to find supervised opportunities for these children to help or mentor others. You might look for ways of pairing them with physically disabled children who may need help being fed, played with, or pushed through the hallways. Another possibility is assigning these students to work with younger students in supervised settings. Tutoring, teaching, or entertaining are viable goals for these interactions.

8) THEY WANT TO HAVE INFLUENCE

Some children live in environments that are too controlled, too unsupervised, or too unpredictable. Too much control imposed by others leads to a push for independence, which is often expressed by breaking rules. Other children have difficulty following directions because they have had too little supervision. Kids worry that they are not lovable when adults provide too little structure. Their fear and anxiety are often at ✳ the root of their misbehavior. "Who are you to tell me?" is a dominant protest from children who have too little structure in their lives. Too much unpredictability leads to confusion and uncertainty. For these youth, breaking rules is a way of trying to make adults be more in charge and reliable. Educators often feel as though they need to "walk on eggshells" around these students who are too often willing to argue. Power struggles are one symptom of this problem.

The main way of determining when "influence" is at the core of misbehavior is to give students who are misbehaving safe opportunities to be in charge. High peer status classroom or school responsibilities should be provided. For some youngsters, cleaning the chalkboard is sufficient, while others may make fine members of a school committee studying an issue of educational importance. Consulting with negative peer leaders in a problem-solving mode often moves their need for power in a more positive direction.

Along with giving students opportunities to be in charge, we should also involve them as directly as possible in decisions that will affect them. The benefits of this idea were demonstrated by Geller and his colleagues (1996), who worked with two groups of pizza deliverers. Participants in one group were told to wear safety belts, while participants in the other group simply discussed the importance of driving safely. The workers in the latter group not only increased their seat-belt use, but they also used their turn signals more frequently than the other group. Geller concluded that "safe driving has typically been a top-down approach by government, and it doesn't lead to generalization of safety behavior. . . . Our research demonstrates that a 'bottom-up' approach involving people in the safety process for one behavior is more apt to spread to other behaviors." This "bottom-up" approach is equally effective with difficult students.

Challenge: Students who misbehave to achieve influence need structure along with opportunities for their opinions and behaviors to affect what happens to them and others. Be sure that your rules are clear and specific, and that students have ownership by active and meaningful participation in their development. When there are problems in the classroom, seek problem-solving input from difficult students. Finally, identify as many high-status classroom or school "jobs" as possible and be sure to assign these for purposes of prevention. Do not wait for these students to "earn" the privilege of a high-status job. It is better to give it to them and then make continuation depend on demonstrated responsible behavior.

9) THEY WANT TO EXPRESS ANGER

Frustration and anger are common when basic needs are unmet. Discipline problems can often be prevented by providing substitute outlets through which students can express their thoughts and feelings. We advise multiple outlets, including a suggestion box for students to offer ways that they believe instruction and learning can be improved for them. When students are angry, they can be instructed to either write down their angry feelings, tell someone how they feel, draw their feelings, or take a timeout.

Challenge: Identify as many alternative ways to express anger as you can. When you are angry, which of these ways work best for you? Share your suggested methods with students. Invite them to share additional methods that are within the rules and can be used at school. When you become frustrated and angry, let them know. Let them see you handle frustrating situations without resorting to hostility and anger. Bring successful examples of effective anger management to the attention of the entire class.

FOCUSING ON THE FUTURE

We have long espoused the virtue of primarily focusing on long-term behavior change. Doing so helps students learn to do the right thing in the absence of authority. This focus on long-term change becomes possible only when we understand how unmet basic needs drive difficult behavior and then incorporate the many ways that educators can effectively address these needs in our classrooms and schools.

Choosing the Best Discipline Strategy

Whether student change is for the good depends on whether we care about their welfare more than our own.

SINCE THERE ARE MANY, many things we can do when discipline situations arise, our effectiveness largely depends on our ability to choose a response that is appropriate to the situation. For example, if a student is out of control, our primary goal is safety. We are less concerned about changing the child's behavior and more concerned about protecting others from possible injury. By contrast, if a student is constantly doing silly, annoying things to get everyone's attention, our primary goal is finding strategies that meet the student's need for attention while reducing his or her interference with instructional time.

When students are disruptive while we are teaching, we have little time to rationally review our choices and assess our options. In addition, the often conflicting and confusing advice we have been given by "experts" who advocate everything from no structure (Kohn, 1996) to firm obedience (Canter & Canter, 1997; Dobson, 1996) have led many educators to choose interventions that are often based more on habit, desperation, frustration, or random chance than on a rational school of thought. This chapter explores the best ways to evaluate strategies to ensure they are as effective as possible.

When selecting a discipline strategy, the three most relevant variables to consider are (1) its overall effectiveness, (2) the type of misbehavior it is designed for, and (3) how it addresses the reason or cause for the misbehavior. You should also determine whether the strategy would work in a crisis or is more appropriate for short-term or long-term results. Some strategies are designed to work immediately in a crisis situation or to address short-term problem moments (e.g., when a power struggle is at hand). Others are designed to address chronic problem behaviors that must be handled over the long term. To determine whether or not a discipline strategy is worth using, answer the following five basic questions:

1. Does using the method preserve dignity or cause humiliation?

2. Is the method primarily obedience-oriented or does it teach responsibility?

3. How does the method affect a student's motivation to learn?

4. Does the method lead to a commitment to change?

5. Does the method work?

1. DIGNITY OR HUMILIATION?

Imagine the building principal or your current supervisor has joined your class for the day to observe your work. She sees Lonnie acting agitated for unknown reasons. In the middle of your presentation, he becomes distracted and begins to wander around the classroom. Then Joella shows up, late and unprepared for the fourteenth consecutive day. You work hard to keep the kids interested, but at one point your patience grows thin and you make a sarcastic remark. During the feedback session, your principal focuses her feedback more on your sarcasm than on helping you find positive solutions to your problems: "These kids have rough home lives, and you should be more understanding. If you want to be successful in your career, you had better get busy developing new skills. I am assigning you to attend a discipline seminar in town next week to help straighten you out." The session ends brusquely with "have a good day." Would you want to straighten out your discipline techniques or your principal? Would this type of interaction help you, even if you were in need of help?

One key question you should ask about any method of discipline is whether it attacks or preserves dignity. Most people have an easier time evaluating this concept when they are on the receiving end of the discipline method. While youngsters may cognitively process an experience differently than an adult would, their feelings toward it are much the same as an adult's. A short-term solution that leads to a long-term disaster is rarely a good trade-off. In addition, it is nearly impossible to maintain our own dignity when we attack the dignity of our students. Good teachers intuitively know that attacking students even in a momentary lapse of weakness takes something away from themselves.

2. OBEDIENCE OR RESPONSIBILITY?

Obedience-based discipline relies primarily on rewards and punishments to achieve coercion. The adult defines the system and controls the delivery of rewards and punishments with little or no input by the child. While obedience is necessary to some degree, especially when safety is an issue, using methods of obedience as a primary discipline philosophy becomes self-defeating in the long run. Students who never learn how to make good decisions rarely make good decisions as they mature. Rewards and punishments rarely, if ever, work when no one is watching the child. Schools need to teach and emphasize the importance of doing the right thing, regardless of how much supervision is present.

In contrast, responsibility-based discipline relies on setting limits and providing choices and consequences. It places control of behavior on the child by teaching decision-making within a context of accountability. Responsible students are those who make ethical, morally correct choices even when they are not being watched.

3. ARE STUDENTS MOTIVATED TO LEARN?

Effective discipline often requires us to weigh trade-offs before selecting an intervention. The most difficult trade-off is when a technique might stop misbehavior, but also stop students from learning by destroying their motivation. A teacher who terrorizes his students to maintain control is most certainly shutting off their curiosity and creativity—essential elements of motivation. Although punitive methods may occasionally be necessary to safeguard the rights and safety of others, we must severely restrict their use unless we are willing to accept the loss of student motivation as their consequence.

Motivating students to learn and sustaining that motivation is difficult even when students are relatively well-behaved. Effective discipline does not interfere with and may actually increase motivation. We must expect students to follow rules and to limit distractions while we establish our classrooms as places of curiosity, creativity, and high energy.

4. ARE STUDENTS COMMITTED TO CHANGE?

Think about the changes you hope to make in your own life. Do you want to quit smoking, spend more time with your children, or catch up on your reading? As much as you want these to happen, they are difficult to achieve, even when you are committed to changing. As we noted in Chapter 2, our desire to change is a hopeless one without a firm commitment. Willpower is not nearly as important as a commitment to change. If we cannot easily change our own behavior with a personal commitment, how can we help students change their behavior without their commitment? The answer is obvious: we cannot. Although commitment does not guarantee a positive change, lack of one guarantees failure. We must always ask ourselves if our interventions lead to or begin the process of the student forming a true commitment to change.

5. DOES THE METHOD WORK?

Effective methods of discipline should end undesirable behavior and begin the process of making better choices. While this seems obvious, most schools and treatment centers persist in using certain ineffective methods. Sometimes, professionals know that a method will not work, but they do not know what else to do. They need to do *something* (even if it will not work) for fear that doing nothing sends an uncaring message to the misbehaving student and sets a poor precedent for other students. Regardless of our reasons for using a discipline method, we must ask ourselves whether or not the strategy works.

However, we do not recommend abandoning a technique that does not seem to work after one try. It often takes persistence before a technique leads to positive results. Try any strategy at least five times or for two weeks before discarding it, but do not waste your time with it if there is no improvement after half a dozen tries or several weeks.

The unconventional discipline methods provided at the end of the chapter will expand your repertoire of new techniques to try when handling student misbehavior.

THREE KINDS OF STRATEGIES

There are three kinds of situations that call for interventions: crisis, short-term, and long-term. Crisis strategies are concerned with restoring order when chaos occurs. The primary goal is to ensure safety and survival. Short-term strategies are designed to defuse classroom escalation and to ensure that power struggles are handled effectively. Long-term strategies have a more preventive focus, in that the educator learns why students misbehave and what to do to make school sufficiently satisfying so that misbehavior is unnecessary.

CRISIS STRATEGIES

In the 1950s, at the beginning of the cold war, schoolchildren had to practice air-raid drills in preparation for nuclear attack. Typically, the ringing of a special bell or siren was the cue for all children to hide under their desks with their hands over their heads. Of course, if a nuclear bomb had fallen anywhere near one of these classrooms, all of the desks and the students under them would have been vaporized. Yet for children going through these drills, the desk provided a sense of security that was mixed with terror. Getting under it provided the child with a concrete action in the face of events happening outside his or her control. Students were being prepared to handle a crisis, albeit not very successfully. Crisis strategies like the one described above are designed to prepare us in the best possible ways to handle events beyond our control. Some are actually effective, while others do little more than offer an illusion of control, which at least provides a sense of security. Sometimes both we and our students respond better in a crisis just by believing everything is under control.

Elements of a crisis plan. Just as fire drills prepare us to handle a fire we hope never happens, we would be wise to anticipate likely behavioral problems and be prepared to handle them adequately as well. Crisis plans are designed to address classroom or school moments in which events need to be handled on the spot. Preparing for a possible crisis involves studying the dynamics of the situation and practicing probable responses.

Remind yourself that you are not trying to solve the problem. That comes later. You are trying to stop the crisis or keep it from escalating.

Determine what crises you might face. What kinds of crises might you expect, given the students you teach (their ages, backgrounds, and experiences) and the environment you teach in: a fight, a student banging his head against a locker, a gun being pulled, a student going ballistic in class?

Determine if you would need help. Who will help you, and how will you get the help you need? You may need an administrator, a counselor, a police officer, a parent, or another person or resource. Know who is available. Have a backup "helper" identified in case your primary resource is unavailable.

Determine how you will quickly get the help you need. Develop a process in your classroom for delivering messages of urgency to others. Do you want a student to deliver a message to the office, or are there other means available? We have found that identifying a special pass as a "crisis alert" pass is a good way to call for help while minimizing the risk of escalating the crisis. A student can be selected as the "errand runner" during a crisis.

Identify what you want the other students to do. If the situation is escalating to the point where the safety or welfare of others is endangered, you may need to have the class leave the room while you stay with the student in crisis. If this becomes necessary, where do you want your class to go, and how will they get there? Can they remain and ignore the crisis situation? Will they need practice in learning how to respond? Do you have activities in reserve to occupy their attention?

Identify what you need to do. How will you respond during a crisis? This part of a crisis plan may include many strategies, but should address the following concerns. First of all, you will need to focus on the crisis at hand. You will definitely need to stop teaching. A true crisis is serious enough to warrant your full attention and resources. Be prepared emotionally for what might come next. Center yourself and focus. Bring all of your internal resources to red-alert status. Be prepared mentally so that you can choose the best strategy based on thought rather than emotion.

After the crisis, try to determine what caused it. If you know why the student was in crisis, you have a better chance of identifying short- and long-term strategies for future use. Ask the student for suggestions: "The next time you find yourself in a situation like this, how can I be most helpful to you, without giving up my responsibilities to you or the class?"

Example of a crisis strategy. Fights are one of the most common crises that occur in schools. If an educator happens upon a fight, he or she can expect an audience to form around the combatants in seconds. There will be students in the audience who are closest to the action and as pumped up on adrenaline as the combatants themselves. The observing students who are farther from the fight are more likely to be less emotionally involved. The educator chooses three or four observing students who are farthest from the fight, taps them on their shoulders, and gives each a specific direction for getting help. The educator then moves closer to the action, pauses when he or she reaches the third or fourth row from the fighters, and asks the best sources in this audience to identify who is losing the fight.

Using this knowledge to advantage, the educator loudly shouts a specific direction to the loser. For example: "Jerry, this is Ms. Lee, a teacher. Fighting is against the rules. Move away this minute. Hustle, before there's more trouble." Most students who are losing a fight are looking for a reason to get out, but they will not leave on their own for fear of losing face. Knowing this, the prepared educator can often more easily distract the loser and then deal with the other student. By that time, help has often arrived.

Finally, the educator should keep in reserve a special, distracting sound or action that he or she uses if the fighters are so involved that neither hears what is said. The teacher can yell the distracting sound, blow a whistle, or even throw cold water on the fighters. Notice that the plan does not include trying to figure out the reason for the conflict at this time, or worry about whether it will happen again. In crisis intervention, the only goal is to stop a serious behavior problem.

Preparing your class for a crisis. Crisis strategies are needed to handle volatile situations. To the extent possible, they define in advance what roles each group or person will have during a crisis. After the crisis has ended, the teacher may involve some or all students in soliciting ideas for preventing them in the future. For example, Nathan has a history of becoming easily agitated and suddenly banging his desk, tipping his chair, throwing his books, and running around the room. The teacher works with all of the children, including Nathan, to define procedures:

1. She reassures and reminds all children before the first or another outburst that she will handle whoever is having "a difficult day."

2. She shares specific, acceptable things that students can do if they are having a difficult day (color your feelings, write down your thoughts, sit in a quiet chair).

3. She lets everyone know what to do if anyone is having an extremely difficult day. For example, she reminds the students that if anything is ever thrown in class, they are to duck and get out of the way. She gives students permission to move themselves to another location. She arranges a special code word with the class and lets children know that the student responsible for running errands should take a special pass to the office for help when he or she hears the code word. Finally, the teacher gives the class a strategy it can use if everyone has to leave because of out-of-control behavior: "If I ever say the word _____, then everyone is to act very grown up, quickly form a line, and leave class. [Name of student who runs the errands] will take the pass to the office for help."

4. She practices crisis strategies with her class.

5. She posts crisis procedures in her classroom.

SHORT-TERM STRATEGIES

Short-term strategies are designed to stop misbehavior while preserving the dignity of the student and teacher. The goal of short-term strategies is to redirect the energy of the class back to instruction so that little time is lost. The following scenarios show short-term strategies in action.

Sam, a 14-year-old student with strong needs for attention and control, challenges his teacher, Ms. Flint, by loudly asking, "How many times have you had sex with your husband?" The teacher is momentarily startled, and the brief silence that follows is interrupted by Sam's interpretation: "You're just ignoring me, aren't you?" Unexpectedly, she responds, "No, Sam, I'm not ignoring you. I was just counting!" There are no further challenges from Sam in that situation.

Shania, a high school freshman, reminds her teacher that he cannot make her do her work. He calmly ponders the challenge and answers, "You are probably right. The real question is not whether I can make you do the work, but whether you can make yourself do it. I trust you will."

LeRoy lewdly challenges Mrs. Robertson in the middle of class: "What would you do right now if I pulled my pants down and showed you what I got?" She answers, "I'd tell you to hurry up because we've got a lot of other things to do."

Short-term strategies are used to defuse a power struggle with a youngster who is pushing your buttons. A typical situation starts over something minor, but before long has careened out of control. It is not unusual for the student to be ordered to the principal's office. The student rarely takes responsibility during the power struggle and never acknowledges that he or she is to blame for it. Let us face reality: the student is not going to become reflective after being tossed out of class and say, "You know, teacher, you are absolutely right. I have been really inappropriate today, and maybe I will develop an action plan at the office. Maybe I ought to get a few detentions as well." Much more often, the student will kick a chair, make offensive comments, or toss things on the way out, creating a bigger problem. Worse yet, he or she usually enters the office with a far more pleasant demeanor, making it appear as though the teacher has overreacted.

Wood and Long (1991) have discussed the effects of the conflict cycle in which angry youth recreate their feelings in others. If we are to work effectively with difficult youth, we must continually be on guard against counter-aggressive behavior, also known as the desire to get even. Because difficult youth believe the world is a hostile place, they behave in a way that triggers hostility in others. Their beliefs are confirmed when they are given the familiar, hostile response. Tierney, Dowd, and O'Kane (1993) have noted that educators and youth workers "must have skills to maintain a calm, positive effect, even when the youth is engaging in verbally abusive behaviors, and to respond with frequent expressions of concern and empathy" (page 45). The combined skills of caring and defusing hostility without anger will interrupt the conflict cycle and often force the youth to consider alternative, prosocial behavior. Short-term strategies are designed for this purpose. They are meant to stop inappropriate behavior in a classroom while preserving the dignity of the student and teacher. They are also intended to preserve the integrity of the group learning situation. In addition to stopping the problem behavior, short-term strategies have four goals:

1. **To respond with dignity to offensive student behavior.** The educator needs to take the high road. We are the professionals, and it is imperative that we respond as such. Becoming angry and hurling offenses back at the student only serve to keep the power struggle alive. It is helpful for educators to realize that all students "have tenure." If they are gone today, they will probably be back tomorrow. Fighting back will only make it harder to work with the student when he or she returns to class.

Short-term strategies provide ways of standing up to attacks without fighting back.

2. **To respond in a way that preserves your own dignity.** The educator must present him- or herself as tough enough to handle the problem. The educator cannot look timid or ineffectual in front of the class.

3. **To keep the offending student(s) in class if at all possible.** Students who are sent out of the classroom for discipline fall further behind academically. While they are gone, they are missing more information. If they remain in class, there is a chance that they will redirect their attention in a more appropriate way. We want to make it as difficult as possible for students to reject their education. Classroom teachers also want to let offending students know that, with rare exceptions, they are capable of handling difficult behavior. Sending a student to the office gives the power and authority to the administrator, taking it away from the teacher. Other students also feel reassured of their safety when they witness an effective adult intervention. However, when behavior is dangerous, excessive, or continually disrupts the learning process, the best choice *can* be to send a student out of the classroom. Many teachers can work out arrangements with colleagues in which disruptive students are sent to each other to provide both parties a timeout.

4. **To model and teach an alternative to aggression.** Every time an educator successfully defuses inappropriate student behavior in a manner that preserves dignity, he or she also succeeds in modeling effective techniques to students. In this era of impulsive and aggressive behavior, we have an important role to play in showing students how to handle "button-pushing" behaviors.

Short-term strategies can be used in all situations, but they are particularly necessary when the youth is involved in group activities. There is a complex dynamic in a group situation that must be managed. The adult needs to focus on preserving the safety and integrity of the group by stopping the inappropriate behavior, maintaining the youth's dignity, and commanding respect from the youth and others in a situation that could escalate out of control. There are many effective short-term strategies. Here are a few of our favorites:

"I" messages. This particularly effective short-term strategy can be used in numerous situations. The "I" message assertively *and* respectfully tells the youth what he or she did, how you feel about it, and what you need from the student. "I" messages can be used in individual and group situations. To imagine how you could use an "I" message, think of a student who says or does things that you find offensive. Use the following conversational structure to confront the student's behavior:

1. When _____ (define the behavior specifically),

2. I feel _____ (tell how you feel)

3. because _____ (give a reason that shows how teaching/ learning is negatively affected).

4. What I need is _____ (set limits).

An example:

When I see people grab things from each other,

I feel sad

because that often leads to fighting.

What I need is for Ryan and Theo to either stay where they are and stop or to move to other chairs away from each other.

The private three-step. This strategy should be used on an individual, one-on-one basis with a student who regularly disrupts class:

1. Use an "I" message.

2. Say: "Are you aware that when you do _____, it makes it hard for me to teach and for others to learn?"

3. Say: "Do you think this behavior is going to change by tomorrow?"

If there is no change the next day, then the follow up continues:

4. Say: "I didn't notice much change today. Usually, when students do _____, they're trying to tell the teacher that either they hate the teacher, the work is too hard, or they are trying to impress their friends. What are your thoughts?"

PEP (privacy, eye contact, and proximity). This method involves getting close to the student; making eye contact (when possible); and privately setting a limit, offering a choice, or giving a consequence. This method is effective because it preserves dignity while enabling the educator to be firm. It works best when it is combined with moments of appreciation that are delivered in the same way and when the educator frequently cruises through the room so that physical proximity with all students is part of his or her teaching style.

Nonverbal PEP. The use of index cards and Post-it® notes provides a good alternative to verbal forms of PEP. Index cards or Post-it® notes should have words or phrases on them that convey either statements of correction or appreciation. Separate cards can say such things as "thanks," "way to go," "please chill," or "stop." Cards or notes can use pictures or colors, such as a stop sign or a green or red light to convey the message to younger children.

LAAD. When a student is more agitated or challenging, we recommend trying the LAAD strategy. This acronym stands for listening, acknowledging, agreeing, and deferring. In our experience, its skillful use is 90% effective in defusing a power struggle. The escalating scenario described below shows how this technique works:

1. **Listening:** "You must be upset, Luis, and right now you are in no mood to listen. I'll respect that." If Luis persists, go to:

2. **Acknowledging:** "Luis, if I understand you correctly, you're telling me that you're not planning to do what is asked. Did I get that right? . . . Thanks for letting me know your plan." If Luis persists, go to:

3. **Agreeing:** "Luis, you are right about that. Neither I nor anyone else can make you do what you don't want to do. I can tell you feel very strongly about this and aren't ready right now to listen. I'll respect that." If Luis persists, go to:

4. **Deferring:** "Luis, this just isn't the time for us to continue because we're headed for an argument that will make one or both of us look bad. Neither of us wants that, so let's put it away until later." If Luis still persists, give him the option to leave the class. "Luis, we need to get back to work, and I hope you'll join us. But if you need to think more about this at the office for a few minutes to settle down, let me know." If necessary, call security or the administrator for assistance.

LONG-TERM STRATEGIES

As we stated in Chapter 4, working successfully with difficult youth requires an unflagging belief in the capacity of human beings to change. The wise, caring adult refuses to give up and understands that he or she can influence behavior by offering genuine moments of appreciation and support. Recent research noted that teachers fail to recognize 95% of all appropriate behaviors. The significance of this finding is profound. It suggests that all educators should try to find several additional moments every day in which they notice accomplishments, identify behaviors they admire, and focus on small gains in a targeted behavior. Many teachers who make a targeted effort to share positive, interactive moments with challenging students have reported substantial improvements in the students' behavior.

It is just as important to focus on specific behavior when you discipline a student as when you praise the student's achievement. When educators need to correct student behavior, they should focus on the specific behavior while providing alternatives that explain the personal and social benefits of responding in a more prosocial way. For example: "Wayanne, I can listen to what you want much better when you talk to me rather than yell at me."

Long-term strategies can grow from a basic needs paradigm (Brendtro, Brokenleg, & Van Bockern, 1990; Glasser, 1986; Maslow, 1968; Mendler, 1992), in which educational experiences and interactive moments are guided by the strengthening of each need. (See Chapter 5.) Long-term strategies require that educators understand and be guided by these basic needs when they arrange classroom experiences and learning activities. For example, an educator can search for ways to increase a sense of belonging by arranging activities that require students to do meaningful things together. Structuring cooperative learning activities is one way of addressing the need for belonging.

An educator guided by the students' need for competence and mastery might involve youth in concrete projects that contribute to the community. Having high expectations while targeting a specific goal can help ensure the success of such projects. For example, incarcerated youth under the guidance of Peter Finch at Oatka Residential Center in New York state created a historic calendar of the surrounding area. To complete the project, these young adults read about the area, visited houses, learned about the architecture of area buildings, and recreated significant historic events through plays. Although many of these youth were barely literate, their high level of motivation and enthusiasm for learning was evident.

Efforts to help our difficult students develop a stronger sense of autonomy, influence, and generosity can be both formal and informal. Students can participate in many aspects of the school experience, such as making rules, deciding on procedural issues, and solving problems as they arise. A greater sense of autonomy can be encouraged by asking students for their opinions and by at least occasionally deferring to their opinions and knowledge, particularly when there is little at risk. Asking students for their ideas ("What do you think about _____?"), carefully listening to their answers, and implementing their suggestions when appropriate will increase their sense of autonomy. For example, "Clarissa, the class seemed bored today. What do you think would make things more interesting?" Students' desire to show generosity can be reawakened by providing opportunities for them to help others through community service initiatives or as a partner in a classroom.

In addition to addressing basic needs, long-term strategies should also consider the in-school and out-of-school factors that affect behavior. For example, many students experience overwhelming stress in their lives. This stress can significantly affect their behavior and academic achievement. As educators, we must have the courage to help our students handle their stressful lives even when the strategies for doing so may be unpopular with our peers. For example, a number of teachers at our workshops have quietly, almost secretly, shared the fact that they have found relaxation techniques, such as guided visualization, to be very effective in helping a child relax and in promoting a calmer classroom that is more conducive to learning.

A five-year study reported in *The Journal of Criminal Justice* (Bleick & Abrams, 1987) investigated the effects of using transcendental meditation in a maximum-security prison. Inmates who learned the technique experienced significant reductions in stress, aggression, and mental disorders. Violence in the prison decreased, and the rate of return among participating inmates was 30–35% less than for four other treatment groups. Similar studies have noted equally impressive results. Rozman (1994) has argued that many hyperactive children are so sensitive that they simply cannot handle the huge number of stimuli constantly bombarding and overwhelming them. She has discovered that the practice of meditation helps them concentrate, focus their sensitivities, and reduce their hyperactivity.

Although we do not regularly practice meditation techniques nor specifically endorse them, schools should be unapologetic when they do things designed to change the person within so that he or she will be more peaceful, productive, and successful. A 1993 American Psychological Association report on violence concluded that school programs that teach social and emotional skills like managing anger, negotiating, adopting another child's perspective, and thinking of alternative solutions to disagreements were particularly effective in reducing violence. These are all long-term programs in that they require repeated presentations, practice, and curriculum time in order for them to work. The positive results of these programs, however, are also likely to be more lasting.

The most important long-term discipline strategy is for students to learn how to be responsible and to make responsible choices on their own. Self-discipline is the most important trait to develop within a child. The best tools for developing responsibility are using limits, offering choices, and providing consequences.

UNCONVENTIONAL DISCIPLINE STRATEGIES

In our book *Discipline with Dignity* (1988), we offered several methods that we referred to as "creative discipline for out-of-control students." Eleven years later, many of these methods are even more relevant and necessary due to the many problems presented by challenging students. Designed to confront chronically disruptive students, most of these methods provide both short-term relief for problem behaviors that disrupt learning as well as long-term benefits. The unfamiliar responses offered by unconventional methods often help lead students to new patterns of improved behavior.

Using humor and nonsense. Write down various jokes, phrases, sayings, and statements that you find funny or nonsensical. Try to include in your list some that are certain to get a rise out of your students. At least once a day for one week, respond with one of your "funny" statements when a student behaves disruptively. For example, as Jack comes late to class for the tenth day in a row, tell him wryly, "Jack! Did you know that Peter Piper picked a peck of pickled peppers?" You'll likely notice a reaction very different from the one you would have received if you had asked again for his pass.

Agreeing with refusals. When students refuse to cooperate and they remind you that there is nothing you can do about it, or when they say offensive things to assert their power, agree! For example, when Jermaine loudly complains that the class is boring, Mr. Thomas responds by saying, "There's probably some truth to that, and I'm sure you'd rather be somewhere else. Thanks for being here anyway." This method can be paired nicely with having a suggestion box, because the box offers the student an acceptable way of expressing his or her ideas. Another example is provided by Lois, who interrupts class to tell Mrs. Chan that she's not going to stay for detention and that her parents support her decision. Mrs. Chan responds by saying, "Let me see if I understand you, Lois. You are clearly telling me that you are not staying, that it is okay with your parents, and that there is nothing I can do to make you. Is that right?" When Lois says, "Yeah," then Mrs. Chan concludes by saying, "Thanks for letting me know."

Dealing with the "what are you going to do about it?" response. Even after things calm down, many students still wonder what action will be taken with the student who acted inappropriately. It is important to respond to this unspoken question with firmness and respect. After an incident that requires consequences or some form of follow-up, avoid wasting any more class time, by telling all students, "Most or all of you just heard and saw what happened, and I know many of you are wondering what I plan to do about it. But as you know, I don't gossip. So know that as soon as I've thought this over and can best understand from Scott why he's so upset today, I'll let him know. Right now, let's get back to page _____ and continue on."

Answering improbably. Imagine telling a student, "I've had enough. You're going to need to go to the principal until you're ready to rejoin the class with more appropriate behavior." The student responds by looking you square in the eye and saying, "I'm not going, and you can't make me. What are you going to do about it?" Now imagine saying, "I'm going to finish this lesson, put on my diving equipment, head out to the ocean, and swim with the sharks. Want to join me?" How do you suppose he and the other students might react?

Thanking the student for proper behavior before you get it. It is very difficult for even the most challenging student to resist compliance when you have already thanked him or her for doing what you want. For example, when Emil refuses a verbal or nonverbal cue to remove his hat, Ms. Shaw says, "Emil, if you keep the hat on, we both waste a lot of time because I've got to write out a referral and we wind up hassling each other. There are many better ways for us to spend our time here, so I really appreciate your cooperation. Thanks for taking the hat off even though I know you think the rule is stupid."

Showing your own imperfections. Acknowledge your mistakes by stating your lack of perfection loudly and publicly. Apologize when you blow it and know it. Even apologize when you are blamed for something you did not do, but it is clear that an explanation will be of no use (e.g., "I'm sorry that your feelings are hurt. I hope we can have a better afternoon.").

Using audio- or videotape. When problems persist, use taping for teaching purposes. After a class when you have captured an incident or a series of disruptions, meet with the students who are causing the problems. Show them or let them listen to the tape and discuss their feelings about the way they looked to themselves. When given a chance to actually see or hear themselves, students often gain an awareness of their negative impact and are more willing to try something new. Create a new plan that is specific, and meet with the students later to discuss how things are going. Since it is common for people to be distracted when they know they are being taped, it can help to make videotaping more a part of the classroom so that students become desensitized to the equipment as well as the thought of their being recorded. When you are using the videotape for behavioral purposes, you want the student to be able to focus on the content of his or her behavior. Naturally, check with your administrator and perhaps the school's attorney to make sure that your recordings conform to legal standards and regulations.

Throwing a tantrum in a controlled way. A few times during the year at most, a well-timed tantrum that includes jumping up and down, standing on a chair, or even throwing a soft foam material on the floor while raising your voice can be refreshing and renewing. Further, it shows students that your humanness includes visceral, nonviolent but poignant, gut-releasing emotion. Students will take notice unless this becomes a habit. Be sure that you have planned this so that you maintain control over what you do. For example, you might decide that the next time someone asks, "Why do we have to know this?" (after it has already been explained 15 times), you are going to permit yourself to have a "tantrum." Naturally, an excessive amount of this type of behavior leads kids to view their teacher as out of control, and difficult students will enjoy pressing their teacher's "buttons" to watch the show.

Reducing stress. A build-up of stress is often a source of discipline problems. It can therefore be quite beneficial to teach students a variety of ways to increase their frustration tolerance. Our previous work has offered in detail many such methods, including simple breathing methods, guided visualizations, and muscle relaxation activities (Curwin & Mendler, 1988; 1997).

Behaving paradoxically. When students are out of control, irrational, intensely defiant, or locked in power struggles, encouraging them to continue doing what you want them to stop may actually help end their misbehavior. Unlike reverse psychology, this paradoxical method is not "reverse power struggles" based on implied threat or sarcasm (e.g., "Okay, stay out all night! See if I care!"). Instead, paradoxical behavior is designed to take away the attraction of negative behavior because it is not only condoned but also encouraged by the authority figure in a way that is neither sarcastic or threatening. This method can be used to end a crisis event and to respond to chronic problems.

Once the incident is resolved, other strategies can be used to find the source of the problem and prevent it from happening again. Ask the student for advice on how to better handle a similar situation in the future: "Ben, we just had a difficult time together. To be honest, I wasn't sure how to best maintain control of the class and still be there for you. What can I do to help you the next time you act like that and still be a good teacher?" Do what the student suggests the next time there is a serious problem. If the suggestion is something you cannot do, tell the student why, and find something you can do: "Ben, I can't let you wander around the room, but I can let you go somewhere to cool off. Where would you like to go that works for me also?" Another strategy would be using the "two-minute intervention" (see page 97) to help repair any lingering damage between you and the student after a major event.

The following example shows how paradoxical behavior can work: Laura was a first-grader who had climbed under a table and begun barking like a dog, trying to bite the other students' feet. Mrs. Ivey crawled under the table and used challenge and paradoxical behavior to quickly end the outburst. She said in a calm, nonsarcastic tone, "Laura, you are a pretty good dog, but yesterday I saw a first-grade *boy* who was a better dog than you." The challenge of a first-grade boy got Laura's attention immediately. Mrs. Ivey continued by saying, "He was louder."

Laura started barking louder. "He ran faster." Laura became more animated. "He was meaner!" Laura climbed out from the table, put her hands to her waist, and said defiantly, "I don't want to be a dog!" The situation was over. Mrs. Ivey then talked with Laura, calming her down and allowing her to continue with the reading lesson. The episode took only four minutes, no one was embarrassed, and no one, including Laura, lost much instructional time.

The more chronic problem of a student's unwillingness or refusal to work can also be addressed with paradoxical behavior. For example, when Devin has not turned in his homework for the fifth straight week, the paradoxical method would be to assign him "no homework." He is approached and with privacy, eye contact, and proximity told, "Devin, I have decided to respect you and not ask you to go against your values. While I don't understand why you refuse to do your work, your behavior tells me that you are strongly opposed to it, and I'll respect that. Beginning tomorrow, your assignment is to not do the assignment. When you come unprepared, you will get your zero as always, but there won't be any further hassle. Incidentally, coming without your homework is much better than not coming at all. I appreciate that."

This strategy cannot be used to respond to any behavior that is destructive, harmful, or hurtful to the student or others. Be careful not to sound condescending or sarcastic when behaving paradoxically. We suggest that you practice behaving this way until it feels genuine before you use it in the classroom. We also strongly advise you to contact parents and administrators before you use paradoxical behavior because it is an extremely unconventional intervention that can easily be misinterpreted.

By understanding the differences among the three types of strategies—crisis, short-term, and long-term—and by being willing to try unconventional discipline strategies from time to time, the educator is better prepared to handle the many challenging moments created by hurt, angry, and aggressive youth. Crisis strategies help an educator regain control of out-of-control situations. Short-term strategies provide numerous ways of defusing potential power struggles while still preserving dignity. Finally, long-term strategies give educators the hope and tools we need to continue to connect with our challenging students.

Seven Goals for Successful Discipline

The more suffering caused by disciplining, the more likely hatred and alienation will result and the less likely students will be to make good choices on their own.

W E HAVE DEVELOPED seven proven goals to help educators identify or create discipline strategies of prevention that are likely to be effective with challenging students. Sometimes the most effective discipline strategies are those that help to prevent problems so that misbehavior is unlikely to occur. Effective discipline strategies of prevention should:

1. Create a caring classroom.

2. Teach self-control.

3. Promote concern for others.

4. Establish clearly defined limits.

5. Emphasize responsibility rather than obedience.

6. Teach conflict-resolution skills.

7. Combine and network with others.

CREATE A CARING CLASSROOM

Students who challenge our authority need us to be tougher at not giving up on them than they are at pushing our buttons and making us angry. They need to know that we welcome them, warts and all! However, because they are disruptive, only the most masochistic and dedicated educators actually look forward to their presence. It takes much wisdom, optimism, and a creative spirit to continue welcoming disruptive students. We recall a teacher who told Bob, a chronically disruptive student: "Bob, since I haven't yet found a way to help you speak respectfully, I have no doubt that God put you in my classroom to help me become a better teacher. Maybe he's testing both of us to find a way to get along."

Difficult students challenge our security, and their lack of compliance often makes us feel incompetent and inadequate. As a result, being caring and welcoming are long-term goals that require a daily, conscious effort. Many students will eventually respond long after they test our genuineness and persistence. Unfortunately, part of the process includes the hostility cycle (Curwin & Mendler, 1997), in which people who care are tested by those who expect rejection. Because caring for difficult students is draining, using a number of structured practices can help ease the strain.

Most of these methods of caring that can facilitate changed behavior take little time, but must be done consistently over a long period of time. You can show you care by:

- Saying hello or shaking a hand.

- Offering at least one comment of genuine appreciation each day to a targeted student or paying close attention to his or her mood. Notice the student and offer a comment such as, "Louise, you don't look too happy today. How would you rate the day on a scale of one to ten?" If the student gives a low rating, you might offer, "Let me know if you think I can help you have a better day."

- Looking for ways to get the student meaningfully involved in class by deferring to his or her competence. For example, if Leila asks a question, rather than answering her directly, advise her to check with Joey (the targeted student). She is told, "Joey is good at fractions. I'll bet he can help."

- Having a question and comment box in the classroom that encourages students to offer feedback on ways to make the classroom more stimulating. If there is a recurring problem, students can be encouraged to offer solutions to it in this way.

- Calling a student at home periodically to offer feedback, solve a problem, or seek a suggestion.

- Using a two-minute intervention in which you identify one challenging student and give two uninterrupted minutes of your time for 10 consecutive days as an effort to build a positive relationship. Raymond Wlodkowski and Judith Jarnes (1990) offer the following suggestions to improve the effectiveness of this strategy:

1. Share time with the student for 10 days. (Consistently using this strategy over 10 days is more important than the amount of time shared each day.)

2. Find a topic of high interest to the student.

3. Gradually move from teacher talk to student talk.

4. Be naturally complimentary.

5. Be prepared for initial rejection.

- Apologizing after a public "knee-jerk" reaction that may have been provoked by the student: "Lou, I got really upset with you before, but it wasn't right of me to say what I did. Sorry about that."

- Using symbols of emotional support. We know a teacher who has big "hugging towels" in her elementary classroom. She lets her students know that if they are having a bad day and just need to be alone for a bit, they can take a hugging towel and wrap themselves up. A middle school teacher we know keeps a few teddy bears in his class. He tells students that he used to love teddy bears when he was a kid and he still does as an adult. But when he was a teenager, he could not let himself show others that he liked them because he was afraid that they would think he was not cool. This teacher challenges them to borrow a teddy bear if they need some cuddling. If they are worried about what others would think, they can just look at the bears in the room on a gloomy day to brighten their spirits. A high school chemistry teacher in San Francisco has 53 teddy bears that students can use at any time in class. She reports that many students use them in nearly every class.

- Having class meetings. This is a good forum to encourage discussions about important issues and/or invite students to share appreciations with each other. The teacher can ask students to share their feelings about the class along with answers to the question, "How can we make it better?"

Planning for a caring classroom. Identify a student, group, or class that is difficult to manage. Consider the strategies we suggest and others with which you are already familiar, and then identify which one(s) you can see yourself using to let challenging students know they are welcome.

TEACH SELF-CONTROL

As a culture, we are just beginning to understand the problems of youthful aggression and violence (Curwin & Mendler, 1997). We still have a very long way to go. Teachers are confronted with classrooms of huge behavioral diversity, including students with impulse-control problems. Teachers attending our seminars often acknowledge the widespread presence of students who have been diagnosed with Attention Deficit/Hyperactivity Disorder. For each diagnosed student, most teachers can identify at least three others that they believe also have AD/HD. Child abuse is another serious problem, with repercussions in the classroom. An estimated three million children in the United States suffer from physical abuse. These children are more likely to show a variety of disturbances in their physiology, thinking, and behavior, including hypervigilance as they continually scan their surroundings for danger and overinterpret the actions of others. An innocent bump in the hall may be perceived as a direct threat and warrant an attack.

The presence of violence in the lives of children clearly puts them at greater risk for impulsive and aggressive behavior. As many as half of the children in some violent neighborhoods show symptoms of AD/HD (Brownlee, 1996)! Children who are constantly on guard against violence have a more difficult time learning. They are usually too busy watching the teacher and others for threatening gestures. Do not make the mistake of thinking this is just an inner-city problem. Children from every economic background are being abused or maltreated in ever-increasing numbers.

Increasing evidence suggests that there may actually be changes in the brains of abused or neglected children that affect their behavior. Megan Gunnar (1996) has found that cognitive and developmental delays correlate with irregular levels of cortisol, a hormone released during stress. When present at higher-than-normal levels, cortisol may damage the hippocampus, a region of the brain associated with the control of emotional outbursts. Because many of our young people are experiencing too much stress, teaching stress-reducing skills is a matter of great relevance.

In addition, too many of our students act impulsively, aggressively, and dangerously when their buttons are pushed. Horrifically, the tragic school shootings that have claimed the lives of too many students and the innocence of so many more are but an extreme that is more usually reflected in lower intensity yet educationally intolerable behavior. Students need opportunities to learn and practice nonviolent ways of expressing themselves when they become frustrated and angry. Data suggest that the earlier they learn these skills, the better. For example, Caspi (1996) has been involved in a number of studies on personality development over the last several years, including a longitudinal study of the personality traits of residents of Dunedin, New Zealand. This study began in the early 1970s and has tracked subjects from ages 3 to 21. Participants were initially assessed at age three and divided into five categories, including an "undercontrolled" category (irritable, impulsive, and reckless). Those assessed as undercontrolled at age three were still aggressive and impulsive at age 18. In addition, undercontrolled three-year-olds were more likely at age 21 to meet the criteria for having antisocial personality disorder.

Successful programs teach self-control skills that are practical and realistic, and they provide opportunities to practice those skills. These programs help youth see and experience how their changed behaviors influence what happens to them. Providing behavioral exercises and related homework assignments can be helpful. For example, students can be challenged to practice behaviors such as smiling, nodding, saying hello, sitting up straight, asking a question, raising a hand before speaking, offering a positive comment, and giving a thumbs up.

This approach helped Juan, a youth who scowled whenever he did not understand or was confused, excited, confronted, or introduced. Unfortunately, most of the time others interpreted his scowl as anger. When confronted with his apparent anger, he would always deny it, frustrating staff and youth alike. During a group session, one youth said, "You should see yourself," and then another pulled out a mirror and held it in front of Juan. Juan's scowling intensified until he looked in the mirror and began to laugh. After that moment, whenever Juan scowled, someone would say, "Get the mirror" or just "Mirror," and Juan would respond by identifying how he was really feeling.

In our prior work (Curwin & Mendler, 1997), we have offered many strategies that educators and students can use to promote better self-control. We have included a sampling of these strategies in this book due to the immense importance of the issue. We believe that good self-control is at least as important as good self-esteem. In fact, many educators realize that bullies may like themselves and be viewed by others as having high status. Taken to the extreme, too much self-esteem and insufficient self-control leads to what Prager (1995) calls the development of "barbarians who feel good about themselves." As educators, we must use and teach drug-free strategies for improving our students' self-control.

You can use the following three-step discussion activity to increase student interest in learning methods of self-control:

1. What are some things that people say or do that make you mad? (Expect students to say such things as "taking my stuff," "calling me names," "saying things about my family," "touching me," "not letting me play," "bugging me.")

2. Why do you think people would say or do these things? (If necessary, ask, "Are these people trying to be friends or get you upset?" Based on their answers to the question in Step 1, ask them to consider the following question: "If someone who knows you'll get upset calls you a name, and you hit them and then get caught and get into trouble, who has the power—you or that person?"

3. Let us now look for and learn things we can say and do when we want to keep our own power. (Teach them methods appropriate for their age and understanding. Several examples are offered below.)

Methods of self-control. Effective methods of self-control include the following six strategies.

1. Button pushing: Charlotte Price of Columbus, Ohio, teaches her severely behaviorally disordered (SBD) intermediate-age children to counter the attempts of others to rob them of their power. Whenever she hears or sees a put-down, Charlotte asks the offended student two questions: "Who is pushing your buttons?" and "Are you going to let her or him win?" She finds this to be a powerful "stop and think" mechanism that helps defuse potentially explosive moments. Students usually begin to help each other with these questions when they see their classmates being harassed by others outside of the classroom.

2. PTI: We know a teacher in San Antonio, Texas, who gives each of his early elementary students a button with the letters PTI on it. He instructs them to wear it because it gives them the magical "power to ignore." If anyone bothers them, all they have to do is point to their button and say, "I have the power to ignore, and I'm using it!"

3. Debuggers: Karen King of Berea, Ohio, presents this list of "debuggers" to her first-graders. The children then practice each of the steps so they understand the strengths and limitations of each:

1. Ignore.

2. Move away.

3. Use "please" and "I" messages ("I" messages have been discussed and presented in depth in Chapter 6).

The following three-step variation on the strategy is taught by Amy Kleissard of the Pine Richland School District:

a. When you _____ (tell the other person what he or she did),

b. I feel _____.

c. So I _____ (what I want to see happen). Example: "When you took my chicken nuggets, I felt mad. So I've decided that unless you give them back or buy me new ones, I'm not playing with you at recess." Amy teaches her kids to "tell them how you feel and make a deal!"

4. Talk firmly but friendly.

5. Get adult help.

4. The STAR method: Students can be taught to Stop, Think, Ask, and React when something happens.

5. Respond with a simple word or sound: When someone says or does something hurtful, say "ouch."

6. Teach relaxation strategies: Breathing, guided imagery, and nonreligious forms of meditation (in a public school) can be very effective ways of helping students increase their capacity to manage stress. Many studies have linked good mental and physical health to effective stress management.

Planning to teach self-control. Identify common student behaviors that reflect a lack of self-control. You might focus on students who are emotionally volatile and explode often or with little provocation. Identify specific strategies that you can use to help these students develop better self-control.

PROMOTE CONCERN FOR OTHERS

Some students have shut down their ability to care for others. They are unable to assume another's perspective because they are emotionally disconnected from other people. As we have noted in the previous chapter, these are often deeply wounded children who have been hurt by those who are supposed to love them. As protection against further pain, these children reject or hurt others before others can hurt them. They are at higher risk for criminal activity because they have emotionally retreated and spiritually withdrawn from others. In our work with many youth who have learned not to care, we have found that they can learn or relearn to make positive connections. To do so, they need to be given opportunities to serve others in a way that shows them how they can positively affect the lives of others through their choices and actions.

In supervised settings, these students need to be in charge of activities and events that other people depend upon.

In particular, we recommend peer helping programs that make the troubled youth the helper. When school discipline programs are being reviewed, we have seen some of the worst-behaved students become thoughtful and responsible committee members. An additional benefit is that they are the real experts about discipline. They know all the rules, all the ways to get around the rules, all the consequences, and often all the measures that might make them less likely to misbehave. Within the classroom, each teacher can encourage concern for others in many ways. We encourage the development of "problem-solving teams," in which all students are assigned to a peer group that supports each of its members when a problem occurs. Unless the problem involves danger, students are guided and encouraged to try to find a solution with their teammates before informing the teacher.

Teachers can also encourage students to be helpers every day and can establish structured methods to make this happen by identifying which students can be helpers for specific activities. For example, the following questionnaire can be used or adapted to provide you with information on your students. Students can be asked to write or draw their answers to the following incomplete sentences:

1. Something I do at home or outside of school that I am good at is _____.

2. Something I do at home or outside of school that I need help with is _____.

3. Something I do at school that I am good at is _____.

4. Something I do at school that I need help with is

   _____.

The educator can then compile a list of class "talents" to share individual student strengths with the class. With younger children, this list can be posted in the classroom. A more subtle approach is usually necessary with older students. For example, you could list groups of older students under categories of talents: four children may be listed as being good at math, while three others could be listed as being good at organizing their desks. All students are advised to check with one or more of those students for help with math or clutter before they ask the teacher for help. With younger children and those who have difficulty paying attention or learning, the teacher can create the categories and have students select from among them. A related option is to establish a "Yellow Pages" directory with categories of services or resources and a listing of students in the class under appropriate categories.

Planning to promote a climate of concern for others. Identify those students who seem to lack a conscience or a sense of remorse, and give them opportunities to care about others. This care can be elicited through classroom activities and instruction that help these students realize they can make positive differences by influencing others. Think of at least two individual experiences that you can provide regularly for this type of student and two total group processes that promote caring.

ESTABLISH CLEARLY DEFINED LIMITS

Good discipline requires that students understand the rules and that they connect the rules to important educational values. In Chapter 2, "The First R," we discussed the connection between limits (rules) and choices. At a classroom or schoolwide level, educators can identify the values or principles that they consider essential to the teaching and learning process, and use them to develop limits and choices. Rules that are based on values that students recognize are generally more effective because students know not only what to do but why they are expected to do it. These classroom or school values and principles may be different from personal values. For example, although a student may personally value and thrive on competition, he or she may need to cooperate with others to learn most effectively.

Educators establish the foundation of their discipline program and motivate students to stay within the limits by showing how rules and values are linked. Examples of values that are consistent with the goals of education and learning are as follows:

1. School is a place where people learn.

2. Students should be and feel safe at all times.

3. Cooperation is preferred to conflict.

4. Everyone is responsible for helping others.

5. Racism, bigotry, sexism, and other biased behavior are not acceptable.

Conway High School in Conway, South Carolina, is an example of a school that has connected values with rules. The importance this school placed on valuing cooperation over conflict and having students help each other led to a "Taking Care" paradigm in which each class developed rules that fit three categories: taking care of yourself, taking care of each other, and taking care of this place. An example of one classroom's Discipline Plan is reprinted below.

DISCIPLINE WITH DIGNITY PLAN

Take Care of Yourself:

Be on time.

Have necessary materials.

Be confident.

Be truthful.

Stay on task.

Take Care of Each Other:

Be respectful by not using put-downs, touching,

pushing, etc.

Smile and be friendly.

Help others.

Encourage others.

Be understanding.

Understand when mistakes are made.

Take Care of This Place:

Put papers in recycle bins.

Keep your work area clean.

Pick up paper and trash even if it isn't yours.

Keep books, bags, etc., under chairs.

Take good care of textbooks.

Planning to develop limits (values and rules). The keys to developing rules that work are to define them by connecting them to one or more educational or social values, to communicate the benefits of following them to your students, to align your behavior so that it models the values you are promoting, and to involve students in the rule-making process so they take ownership of the rules.

EMPHASIZE RESPONSIBILITY RATHER THAN OBEDIENCE

Students learn responsibility by being given opportunities to make decisions, take action, and experience the consequences of their choices. When they are involved in proposing classroom rules and choosing consequences, their commitment to these rules and consequences deepens and they learn greater responsibility because they see the connections between expectations, actions, and consequences. Consequences are the natural result of choices, both positive and negative.

We have long advocated that educators do the *right* thing rather than the same thing when students break rules (Curwin, 1992; Curwin & Mendler, 1988, 1997; Mendler, 1992). Because people learn differently, the challenge in discipline is the same as in instruction: to give each student what he or she needs. Students are informed that the rules include consequences. If a student makes a mistake by breaking a rule, then one or more of the consequences will occur. However, asking a student to help you select the consequences can help ensure that the consequences will actually help him or her avoid breaking the rule again.

Consequences are categorized and shared verbally, in writing, or both. The goal is for students to make natural or logical connections between their mistakes and the corrective actions. Because it is not possible to anticipate every imaginable offense or to detail every possible consequence, we advise teachers to develop a list of specific consequences but also include a final category called "other." This allows them to create consequences as needed. The following list of possible consequences can be developed and shared with students:

1. **Reminder or warning:** Disapproval may be conveyed verbally or nonverbally.

2. **Conference:** The student is reminded about his or her problem behavior, and expectations are reinforced. A plan for improved behavior may be needed if the student seems unsure about how to meet the expectations.

The conference can be held with the teacher, administrator, or both.

3. **Parent involvement:** The educator seeks cooperation of the parent or guardian in helping the student move toward positive behavioral change.

4. **Peer mediation:** The participants in a dispute meet with a neutral peer or peers in an effort to reach a settlement that will accommodate their needs.

5. **Restitution:** When school or personal property has been damaged, stolen, lost, or destroyed, the student may be held responsible for replacing the items or paying the cost of the item.

6. **School or community service:** This requires that the student make some form of contribution to the school or community, such as making repairs to the school or local church or cleaning graffiti from buildings. Parental agreement is usually required.

7. **Time-out and in-school suspension:** The student receives his or her educational program at another site in school that is either quieter or more highly supervised. The goal is to offer the student a chance to cool down emotionally and/or to reflect deeply upon his or her poor choices before meeting with the educator to develop a plan for more responsible behavior. Reflection does not usually happen automatically. Another student or educator usually needs to begin the process by asking questions or structuring a plan for a change of behavior.

8. **Written behavioral contract:** The contract describes the behaviors that need to occur, the procedures for following the rules, and the privileges or consequences that will be earned when rules are either followed or broken.

The contract is a collaborative effort between the school staff and the student, and may include parents or others who are influential in the child's life. Most written contracts fail when the student views the document, not his or her change in behavior, as the final product. Before the student puts the plan into writing, the educator needs to ensure the student's commitment by asking such questions as, "Will you really do this?" and "When do you expect your plan to begin working?" and to help the student plan for contingencies by asking, "What will you do if Matt provokes you by calling you a coward?" and "What are some other consequences we may need just in case this plan doesn't work?"

9. **Arrest and prosecution:** This consequence occurs when criminal laws are broken. Obvious instances are the presence of weapons and the possession, use, or sale of drugs on campus. Discretionary instances may be fights (since these might be viewed as assaults) or smoking on school property, which could warrant a fine.

While we have focused our discussion of responsibility on consequences, the key in teaching responsibility is to provide opportunities for students to be responsible so that they receive the practice they need. For example, Garrity, Porter, and Jens (1996) noted that bullies modified their behavior when they were allowed to rechannel their power into positive activities, such as becoming active in the safety patrol program. They noted an instance in which a school counselor took aside a fifth-grader who was terrorizing kindergartners and first-graders. The counselor told the boy that someone was picking on the young children and asked the bully to help. In essence, the bully became the guardian. Linda Steinberg at Crane Elementary School in Rochester, New York, provides another example of this strategy in action. She describes an AD/HD child who was regularly inattentive. She privately told the child that many students in class were not listening well and were missing important information. She asked that he listen especially closely to the directions so that other students who were not listening as well could get help from him if they needed it. As a result, this inattentive child became a hypervigilant listener for the whole class.

Planning to emphasize responsibility. Niles Community Schools in Niles, Michigan, has developed a comprehensive discipline plan that includes the key ingredients of principles (values), rules, and consequences. We have included it as an appendix for your reference.

TEACH CONFLICT-RESOLUTION SKILLS

Our society has become less patient and civil as it has adopted an increasingly confrontive, "in-your-face" mentality. We believe we can help students find positive ways of handling the insults and incivility of others. As John Leo editorializes in *US News & World Report* (1996, page 73), "our levels of political, social and commercial discourse are now so low that it is surely time to try restoring civility from the bottom up. The alternative would seem to be an increasingly stupid and brutal culture. A start would be zero tolerance for messages and tactics aimed primarily at degrading and enraging opponents. . . . This new intolerance should apply equally to angry anti-abortion demonstrators harassing doctors at their homes and angry gay demonstrators attempting to degrade the various symbols and trappings of Christianity. Isn't this a modest proposal?"

The strategies offered below have either been taught by us or are widely used in conflict-resolution and peer-mediation programs. In addition to helping students resolve conflicts, they will also help students develop better self-control.

Seven steps to success. Follow these steps with one student at a time.

Step 1: Name the problem.

Step 2: Name what you want to have happen (your goal).

Step 3: Say what you will do (your plan).

Step 4: Say what else you will do if your plan does not work (backup plan).

Step 5: Share your plan and backup plan with someone you trust to see if it makes sense to that person.

Step 6: Follow the plan and, if necessary, the backup plan.

Step 7: Change the plan if necessary.

Five answers to give. Use this strategy with one student at a time.

1. What took place just before the incident that got you into trouble?

2. What happened?

3. Did anyone else see what happened?

4. If we asked that other person what happened, what do you think he or she would say?

5. What could you have done differently?

Two-person problem solving. Use this strategy when two students have been in conflict with each other. Give each student a chance to answer the following questions. After each student answers, encourage the other student to repeat what he or she heard. This will help promote understanding and empathy.

1. What happened? or What's the matter? (Expect each party to get into the "he did/said, she did/said" mode.)

2. Do you see things the same way or differently? (Expect that there will almost always be different versions.)

3. What happened before _____ (the incident)?

4. How do you think he or she felt when _____? (This is an optional question that can promote understanding, but might also divert attention from solving the problem.)

5. Next time you have a problem like this, what else will you both do so you do not get into trouble? (Having both sides write or draw their plan together often replaces conflict with collaboration).

Problem-solving page. In the problem-solving process on the next page, younger children can draw their answers to the questions: What happened? How did you feel? and What could you do next time? It can be expanded to include all of the steps in the two-person problem-solving strategy.

SODA. The SODA process is adapted from the Boys Town Model. It provides a way for considering the *situation*, three different *options*, and the *disadvantages* and *advantages* of each. We like it because it can be applied to situations involving individual, small-group, and large-group problem solving. The teacher usually begins the SODA process by describing the situation and then leading the students through the remaining steps. (See page 117.)

Class planning and problem solving. This strategy should be done with either a small group or with the entire class when a student's chronic misbehavior is creating fear or anxiety. We recommend you do this without the misbehaving student in the room. This is a risky process because it excludes the student,

PROBLEM-SOLVING PAGE

Name: _____

Date: _____

   1. What happened:

   2. I felt:

       The other person felt:

   3. Next time I could:

and should therefore be done only after less extreme measures have been taken. Since the student and his or her parents might object to a discussion being held with others in their absence, it is wise to inform the student and his or her family before using this strategy. For example: "Jim, this afternoon, I'll be meeting with some other students in our class to get their ideas on how you and they can get along better together. I've reserved a spot for you in the library so that you might come up with some ideas of your own. I look forward to hearing your ideas tomorrow." When you meet with the group or class, guide their discussion by having them consider three questions:

1. How do you feel about _____'s behavior?

2. Why do you think (he or she) acts that way?

3. What do you think you could do besides just not liking _____?

Planning to help students resolve conflict. Some of your best ideas for developing a plan for conflict resolution may arise from conflicts in your own personal or professional life that you were able to handle successfully.

Think of a conflict situation in your classroom that is adversely affecting student learning. Based on the actual situation and the number of students involved, choose one or more of the strategies identified above. On a separate sheet of paper, write down how you plan to use each of the strategies.

COMBINE AND NETWORK WITH OTHERS

Seita, Mitchell, and Tobin (1996) point out that many challenging youngsters need a "fan club" of support. Because their intense needs can lead to a roller coaster ride of behavioral ups and downs, they can drain our energy and resources. Educators who want to make a difference might find it helpful to view themselves primarily as service organizers rather than

SODA*

(Situation, Options, Disadvantages, Advantages)

Name: _____

Date: _____

Situation: Describe the problem or situation you are trying to figure out.

_____

_____

Options: Describe three different things you can really do about the situation you have described.

Option 1: _____

Option 2: _____

Option 3: _____

Disadvantages: Disadvantages are things you do not like about the options you have identified. List at least two disadvantages for each of the options you identified.

Option 1: _____

Option 2: _____

Option 3: _____

Advantages: Advantages are things you like about your options. List at least two advantages for each of the options you have identified.

Option 1: _____

Option 2: _____

Option 3: _____

Review the advantages and disadvantages of the options you wrote. Then select the option that gives you the most advantages and the fewest disadvantages. Which option did you select?

      Circle the option number: 1   2   3

If your selection is a solution to the problem situation, make an oral or written plan describing how you will carry out the option you selected. Please use the back of this page.

*Thanks to the Round Valley Middle School in Lebanon, New Jersey, for this form. The SODA process was created by Boys Town in Omaha, Nebraska.

service providers. The goal, then, is to develop a network of people who serve various functions in the difficult student's life. These support people can come from a variety of in-school and out-of-school sources. The in-school network may include classroom peers, older students, administrators, support personnel, and other teachers who care about the student. The out-of-school network may include parents, senior citizens, mentors, police officers, doctors, and mental health professionals.

Ideally, each member of a student's support network has a primary function. For example, an older student may be assigned as a tutor. A senior citizen volunteer who is available for two hours a week might become the child's special friend for part of that time. An administrator or counselor might be chosen as the person the child will go to when he or she has a tantrum. The Big Brothers/Big Sisters of America organization might be asked to contact the child and his or her family in the community. Peers in the classroom may become part of the support network by identifying what they should and should not do to influence the behavior of the targeted child.

Although the task of establishing a support network is rarely finished, the long-term payoff for the considerable time and energy this ongoing effort requires can be dramatic. Efforts to create a support network also create a plan for handling the chaos caused by a child's behavior. Simply knowing who to have the challenging child turn to will help those who work with him or her to relax. The division of responsibilities within the support network usually prevents burnout.

Planning to create a network of support. A good network support plan establishes a framework for meeting the needs of the child and classroom. This framework should include in-school and out-of-school people who can best meet the student's needs.

In summary, success with challenging students is best achieved through practices and strategies that are compatible with each of these seven goals for successful discipline. The time and energy you invest in the prevention of discipline problems will usually lead to less misbehavior and create a positive climate for learning.

NETWORK SUPPORT PLAN

Student's Name: _____

Problems Caused: _____

_____

What you think the child is trying to achieve through the behavior:

_____

_____

The child's strengths that can be built on: _____

_____

In-school supports (identify in-school people who can help during these times): _____

_____

Out-of-school supports (identify out-of-school supports who might be called, such as police, medical personnel): _____

_____

Crisis moments (identify highly disruptive behaviors and proposed actions):

_____

_____

Short-term interventions (identify precursory or early behaviors that occur before things escalate and proposed actions): _____

_____

Long-term interventions (identify strengths that can be further developed or basic needs deficits to be addressed and proposed actions):

_____

_____

8

Special Discipline Problems

Making mistakes is not failing; not learning from them is.

WHILE EDUCATORS FACE many discipline challenges, three specific problems warrant our special attention. Although these problems occur frequently, little information is available on how to handle them:

1. Lack of motivation and its relationship to discipline.

2. Students who have trouble paying attention and the classroom problems that result.

3. The growth and influence of gangs in our schools.

LACK OF MOTIVATION

Students who are hard to motivate are often hard to discipline. Although it is difficult to assess which is the cause of which, the connection is clear. And the problem is growing. Our seminars are increasingly attended by educators who question what to do with students who are not prepared, will not work, and do not care. Those who are both hard to motivate and to control often make us wonder why we should bother with them at all when there are so many others who do care and do want to learn.

In actual practice, many students who behave in these ways or give up are trying to cover their own concerns about being "stupid." They are protecting themselves from the embarrassment of looking dumb in the eyes of their classmates, parents, and selves. Other students find power and control in their refusals to work. They are competent and capable, but their need to be in control is so strong that they use a self-defeating strategy to exert their independence.

Our professional responsibility requires that we teach all students and make our best effort to motivate even those who seem not to care. If we give up on them, they will cause more problems, and be more hurtful, more dangerous, and more costly. Although the answers are not simple, there are many things that educators can do to reawaken motivation in students who have lost interest and perhaps hope. Strategies for increasing student motivation should:

- Emphasize effort
- Create hope
- Respect power
- Provide an appropriate level of challenge
- Build relationships

Emphasize effort. In Chapter 1, we discussed the difference between effort and achievement as a basis for understanding behavior problems. We believe that a focus on effort is crucial to increase achievement, promote learning, and minimize behavior problems among students who are trying to hide their academic inadequacies. Although this focus may be difficult to attain, many classroom techniques can emphasize the value of effort.

Build on mistakes or partially correct answers: Mistakes are potent learning tools when they are used to diagnose rather than evaluate. In school, we can build on mistakes to increase learning when we frame them as part of the learning process rather than as an indication of failure. Madeline Hunter suggested that wrong answers be "dignified" by acknowledging the part that is right. For example: "Lincoln wasn't the first, but you're right about him being president," or "Oscar, you did a great job on four of your answers. They show that you understand the first part of the story. Let's look at how you can improve the next four. Look over my suggestions on the next four, and see how that can make your essay even stronger." In discussions and classroom projects, mistakes can also be used to determine how much more teaching still needs to occur and/or how learning processes need to be improved. For example: "Heather, your mistake helps me understand that I need to explain this concept more clearly. I bet others were also confused. Thanks for the help."

Use "works in progress": Rarely is one's first attempt at anything a final endeavor. Writers usually edit several drafts before submitting a final version. Architects carefully review and revise a design for a bridge many times before the building begins. Accountants review their books carefully. Similarly, it is unrealistic to expect students to do their best work on their first attempt. Effort and learning are enhanced by allowing students to retake tests and revise projects, papers, and experiments based on feedback from the teacher or other students. While curriculum modifications are also sometimes appropriate, simply adding the redo, retake, or revise option lets them know that their efforts can lead to improved achievement.

Naturally, there must be a proper balance between students having opportunities to improve their performance while demonstrating their consideration for others and their responsibility for themselves. Teachers should tell students what they need to do to improve and how long they will have to work on improving the product. A semester's worth of papers should not be accepted one day before grades are due. Teachers must also guard against promoting procrastination and minimal effort on the first attempts.

For example, when teaching in college, one of the authors distributed the final examination on the first day of class and gave the students the entire semester to finish it. They had as many chances as they wanted to hand in their papers for review, and they chose the version they wanted to count toward their grade.

Count improvement officially: Improvement is a sure sign of effort. But because improvement is harder to measure than a test result, it is usually ignored. Nevertheless, part of the official grade should count effort equally to achievement. Separate but equal grading for improvement reinforces the importance of working to one's capacity. Obviously, an increase in test scores demonstrates improvement and can be used as an indicator of effort. In addition, you might brainstorm with your class to identify other indicators that show your students how important their improvement is to you.

Create hope. Perhaps the most common cause of poor motivation is hopelessness. Students who simply do not believe they can master the curriculum or that mastery will improve their lives are the least motivated and most likely to become behavior problems. In truth, children and teenagers *learn to be unmotivated*. All healthy infants are born inquisitive, curious, and "motivated." Those who remain healthy grow to be toddlers who are so "motivated" that their parents have to rearrange their homes by erecting gates and blocking steps. Like a flower that can be nourished to bloom or wilts through neglect, our interests are determined by a blend of talents nurtured by others, along with built-in natural talents and proclivities. This nurturing dynamic is the foundation of all effective interventions, both conventional and unconventional, that build motivation.

Show how achievement benefits life: In the past, many children were motivated by the expectation that if they got a good education, they would get a good job, make money, and have a good life. Today, too many kids do not buy this, and with good reason—good things that should happen don't always. However, the reality remains that, on balance, college graduates do better than high school graduates, who do better than dropouts. Therefore, we need to find new ways to use data that show this reality as a tool. In addition, we need to take special care that students who are not obedience oriented and who do not necessarily trust those in authority can see some connection between what we teach them and how it relates to their lives. They need to see how the explorers like Balboa are relevant today and how solving an equation may relate to the house they live in, the car they drive, or the basketball shot they choose to take. Finally, when students observe and experience people they can relate to doing things that use the information students are asked to learn, the connection between achievement and life benefits can become most real. Effective mentoring programs that bring successful adults into schools and bring students into their workplaces often have this effect.

The problem with these conventional motivational methods for many students is that young people frame time differently than adults do. High school students may see the future as within a month, middle school students as two weeks, and elementary students as three days. Teachers who can find benefits for their students within these timeframes can increase motivation. However, finding benefits depends on knowing the students and their true aspirations—not only the obvious ones, such as having good careers or making money. Benefits need to fit in with their lifestyles and environment—not conceding to them, but expanding from their reality.

One immediate benefit for your students is the joy and love you have for what you teach. Continuously demonstrate with words, actions, body language, and emotion why you love what you are teaching by first identifying and then communicating it. If you do not love what you teach, you will communicate that to your students with the expected result that they will not love it either. Find at least something to love within the subject or do not teach it.

Respect power. Our motivation is largely influenced by our beliefs about our own competence and autonomy or power. Some students find power and control in their refusal to work.

Challenge the refusals respectfully: Students who refuse to work frustrate teachers who care because they make us feel like failures. After unsuccessful efforts, it is not unusual for educators to give up and adopt the attitude that "it's up to Jerome—I need to give my attention to the kids who care!" Giving up is usually a way that we protect ourselves from continued rejection by the student. Instead, the professional approach must always be to find ways of staying personally connected with the student without taking the inappropriate behavior personally. When students refuse to work, we have a better chance of inspiring motivation when we let go of our need to "shape" the students' behavior. It is helpful to identify how their behavior is actually positive so that we can encourage rather than nag. For example, most students who refuse to work but come to class are actually learning much of the information being presented.

Unfortunately, their need for power and control precludes them from showing us that this is happening on a regular basis. Along with the lack of homework, papers, and preparation, these students' test scores may suffer as well, although it is not unusual for them to do quite well on exams. Students who demonstrate their power by refusing to work need to know that their presence is more important than their behavior, even if their behavior has consequences. For example, a teacher might say, "Bill, I know I hassle you a lot about not doing your work, and I'll probably keep doing that because I respect you too much to expect anything less than your best. Most students who won't work are either afraid of failing or are needing to feel in charge. I hope that as you get to know me and this class, you'll feel brave enough to take a chance. Either way, keep coming and keep learning." If necessary, a consequence can follow.

Use short-term gains: Behavior modification programs rely on short-term gain to change behavior. Stickers, stars, charts, auctions, pizza parties, and extra privileges have become standard methods of motivation in most classrooms. Although these approaches may appear to change behavior fast, the change does not last. In fact, there can be serious negative side effects to behavior modification programs that should make us limit their use far more than we do. These include possible adverse effects on internal motivation—"what's in it for me?" games can lead to bribery and replace the desire for mastery with the expectation of tangible gain.

However, there are times when rapid change is necessary. Hurtful or chaotic behaviors need to be changed quickly in order to ensure safety and success. A child who hits others may benefit from a formal behavior modification system that motivates him to stop hitting by helping him realize that he has the power to control himself in the presence of desired incentives. And it is better to offer external incentives to jumpstart and sustain a child's interest in reading than to allow that child to fall far behind his or her peers. However, since all behavior programs that rely on external reinforcement have limited results at best, use them only to change behavior quickly, then turn to more responsibility-based methods to sustain the gain.

Offer real choices: Perhaps the most significant method of motivating is to actually give the power to learn directly to the student. The more say the student has in selecting subject matter, teaching methods, and assessment, the less likely the student will feel the need to demonstrate power in negative ways. The simplest way to have students achieve ownership of learning is to offer them significant choices: "Answer three of these six questions"or "Your work needs to be completed by the end of the day. Would it be best for you to do it now, during recess, or during another time today that I haven't thought of?" Choices can be included in most assignments, projects, papers, and tests. Choices can be given in developing rules, selecting consequences, and defining class procedures, responsibilities and rituals.

Provide an appropriate level of challenge. Finding the right level of challenge is one of the most important tools we have to reach students. Csikszentmihalyi (1990) has demonstrated that when the level of challenge is too low, motivation is lost. Climbing a staircase does not come close to the excitement and challenge of climbing a mountain. Tasks that are too easy are not motivating. And if a student fails at an obviously easy task, the results are significantly more harmful to his or her self-esteem. However, when tasks are too difficult, students give up. Mountains must be created that students believe they can climb. This means that each classroom and subject must be a mountain range with peaks of different heights to ensure a match between the peak and the aptitude of the climber. When challenge matches ability, the conditions are right for students to participate enthusiastically.

Create challenges that can be mastered: In our seminars, we will often challenge participants to find a partner and together count the number of "e"s on a U.S. penny. We give them one minute to complete the exercise. At least 95% do the task, and when we call time, several continue beyond the time allotted. We remind them that they are actually "cheating" when they keep going after we have told them to stop. Naturally, most participants are interested in the official answer, so when we tell them that we do not know the answer because we have never done the task (we would not want to waste our time on a meaningless activity that doesn't benefit life), many groan as if realizing they have been "had." While there is a certain satisfaction for us in this harmless fun, the main point made is that we "motivated" a very large group of intelligent, well-educated professionals to do this "meaningless" activity by giving them an unusual task that could be successfully achieved in a reasonable period of time. Educators can often inspire motivation in a similar way by varying the type of instruction while providing tasks with identifiable outcomes that can be achieved within a reasonable timeframe.

Focus on the learning process: More learning occurs when information is shared in brain-friendly ways (Caine & Caine, 1991; Sylwester, 1995). Teaching processes that affect motivation can be guided by our understanding of "multiple intelligences" (e.g., Armstrong, 1994; Gardner, 1993), "learning styles" (Dunn

& Dunn, 1982), and "preferred learning activities" (Goodlad, 1984, 1990). In addition, we strongly advise teachers to be their own ongoing researchers with their students in some easy-to-implement ways, such as periodic surveys. For example, students can be asked the following:

- Think about something you do or have done in which you are successful. What was it about the situation that helped you succeed? Did other people help? What did they do?

- What does it take to make you succeed?

- What kinds of rules or procedures do you need to help you succeed?

It can also be helpful to keep a suggestion box in the classroom where students can contribute their ideas and thoughts about how the class can be even more fun for them. Let students know that you will try to include their ideas and that you may be consulting with them from time to time about their suggestions.

Build relationships. For years, our books, articles, and training sessions have described how many discipline problems can be prevented by making students feel welcome and included, deepening our relationships with them, and finding ways of preserving our relationships when we need to intervene. Motivation is no different. There will be times when learning is not fun, when the benefits of learning are not immediately relevant to the students' lives, and when learning cannot be geared to an individual's preferred learning style or intelligence. For example, memorizing multiplication tables can be a painful, yet necessary exercise for many students, with little hope of fun and stimulation. When one of our sons was an AP physics student and being similarly challenged by the material, he was actually reassured to hear his teacher advise him and others that they could not yet possibly expect to understand what they were doing because they were still "learning the language" of physics. It would begin to make sense later on.

In these situations, we inspire motivation because of the work we have previously done to establish trust with our students. We make deposits into the "reservoir of goodwill" so that we can make withdrawals when needed. There are times when we must rely on a good relationship ("do it because I'm telling you it is important") to elicit a student's optimal effort.

Empathize with and affirm the student: Challenging students need us to affirm our belief that they are more important than what they do, even while they face unpleasant consequences due to their misbehavior. While limits and consequences are often needed, difficult students need to know that they are wanted. An unmotivated student who persists in being disruptive can be told, "Cleo, I'm embarrassed and disappointed in your behavior. I don't want to look bad in front of everyone and neither do you, so we need to deal with this issue later when we can respect each other's ideas." If the behavior continues: "Cleo, you'll have to leave class if this doesn't stop. I hope you choose to stay because I'll miss you if you go, but if you must leave, come back as soon as you are ready." One of our goals should be to make it as hard as we possibly can for students to choose poor behavior or lack of caring.

PROBLEMS WITH ATTENTION

A parent recently shared the following story: "I asked my son's second-grade teacher why she called me in to talk. I was told: 'Your son never pays attention. He ties his shoe, tries to find something in his desk, looks out the window, ties his shoe again, walks to the pencil sharpener, forgets his pencil, ties his shoe, drops his book, and whispers to his friend; but he never pays attention.' I asked, 'Do you ever call on him?' She said, 'Yes, all the time.' 'Does he ever have the right answer?' I asked. 'Yes, all the time,' she answered. 'Then what is the problem?' I asked. She replied: 'He rarely pays attention and even if he has the right answer, other students are so distracted by him that they can't concentrate.'" This sums up the problem with students who have difficulty paying attention. They may be able to learn, but their behavior distracts other students from learning. To help these students, we need to:

1. Allow them to pay attention in their own way without learning to hate school in the process. In the example above, the student was clearly paying attention—he knew the answers—even as he looked out the window, walked around class, or whispered to a friend.

2. Make arrangements so that their way of paying attention does not keep other students from paying attention as well.

Many of our students have been diagnosed with AD/HD. While this is certainly an accurate diagnosis for some, it is an overused term that reflects a culture increasingly guided by "escalator thinking" toward solutions that are fast, easy, and attractive. People have become increasingly impatient with delays, expecting to acquire experience and information quickly and with little effort. For educators, the end result is that classrooms contain significant numbers of students who are easily distracted, act impulsively, and have attention problems.

Attention Deficit/Hyperactivity Disorder is a physical disability for the student that can become an attitude disability for the educator. Because its manifestations are so annoying and distracting to teachers and students, educators must adapt their approach to provide relief for AD/HD students by addressing their behaviors in a way that increases their motivation to learn even as it minimizes the distraction for other students. Whether students actually have AD/HD—a disorder that is still very difficult to diagnose accurately—is perhaps less important to the educator than being skilled in successfully teaching students who have a hard time paying attention. Because teachers face this reality, we offer many drug-free strategies that have effectively helped students improve their ability to focus.

Believe that students can learn differently, and familiarize yourself with methods of active learning. If you are a teacher in school, you get to walk and talk all day. Having AD/HD tendencies might even be seen as an asset, once your organizational skills are developed. Your strong desire for change helps you move through the classroom, be animated, motion with your hands, even make rapid shifts from one activity to the next that can prevent boredom. Now think about what activities are available to AD/HD students. Chances are, they are asked to spend a considerable part of their time at school sitting at a desk and controlling their impulses to move around, speak, and change activities. It is important to understand that school restrictions and limitations exacerbate this condition.

If students feel unwelcome, then a more serious problem will develop as they begin to hate school and might even begin to hate themselves. Many parents of AD/HD students have become strong advocates for AD/HD children after they have seen their child lose motivation, begin to hate school, and become a discipline problem. The first two steps in being successful with AD/HD students are to show respect for who they are and to develop a positive belief in their future and a tolerance for their needs. Our goal is not to change them, but to help them be more successful, regardless of their attention deficits. It is often helpful to plan and collaborate on program development and expectations with students and their parents. We must never ask students to do what they cannot do or punish them when they try and cannot.

Verify diagnosis. Because many other problems, including depression and anxiety, can cause many symptoms similar to those of AD/HD, accurate diagnosis is important. Tools for making a correct diagnosis include observation, completing professional checklists, and interacting with the student in collaboration with medical and psychological professionals.

Review your expectations and demands. Once the diagnosis is as accurate as possible, review what behavior you can honestly expect from the student. Do not demand what is beyond his or her ability, but do "stretch" what is possible. Present all expectations and demands with care, understanding, and the expressed belief that what you ask for will benefit the student. You can also benefit from the experiences of supportive colleagues by brainstorming with them for strategies that can help the child while allowing others to learn.

Allow alternatives to handwriting. Many AD/HD students have trouble with handwriting. It is as if they think much more quickly than they write, so by the time a thought is on paper, they are five thoughts further down the road. As a result, their handwriting is often illegible and their papers are disorganized, even when they are capable of thinking in an organized way. You can help these students by reducing their need to use handwriting. Curiously, AD/HD students tend to flourish at the keyboard. Assignments done on a computer often need no special restrictions. Another option is to permit students to audio-record their assignments and/or to provide more "hands-on" ways of expressing their knowledge.

Provide a daily schedule of activities. AD/HD students typically have great difficulty at anticipating upcoming events, and tend to have more trouble behaving during transitions. Younger children can benefit from a picture schedule or photos of upcoming activities, while older students can benefit from a checklist of the day's schedule.

Provide a daily assignment sheet. This type of organizer can provide the kind of structure that AD/HD students and their parents need. In fact, it is often best to mail home a copy of the weekly assignment sheet and ask that parents acknowledge receiving it. In this way, both the student and parents know what is expected and when the assignment is due.

Have students keep different-colored folders for each subject. Each class or subject should have a distinctive folder to help students keep organized. The folder should be further organized to define specific tasks (e.g., homework, notes for home, and practice questions).

Identify the lesson's objectives. Many AD/HD students are unable to distinguish the relevant from the less relevant, often becoming lost in the details or background. It is as if they are hypersensitive to the details of each tree while they fail to notice the forest. Some might give an extraneous noise or sound the same importance as the teacher's voice. Therefore, it is extremely important to identify the key concepts or functions of each lesson or story that you want them to notice. For example, you can help AD/HD students by telling them the specific objectives of a lesson and even writing them on the chalkboard. Then ask your students to listen and look carefully for information related to the identified objectives.

Encourage other students to help. Most students with special needs provide opportunities for the teacher to build a sense of community and caring. Since there are some students in every class who are well organized, these students can help others who need help with organization. When involving classmates with a specific student's concerns, teachers must be especially sensitive not to embarrass or point fingers at the student.

Use music or tapes to compete with auditory distractions. Playing background music during individual work time can provide a consistent auditory background for students who are easily distracted by noise.

Allow standing. Some students have a hard time concentrating while seated. We advise allowing these students to stand during "seat work" activities. Providing a boundary such as a music stand or a clipboard usually prevents these students from roaming.

Assign two chairs. The behavior of students who are continually out of their seats and wandering through the classroom can improve when you assign them to two chairs. Their assignments can also be structured so that they do not need to sit in either of their seats for extended intervals. For example, the student is assigned problems one and two at her first desk and is told to pack her books and go to her second desk to complete numbers three and four. When possible, it can be best to have an extra set of books at the other desk. Although not ideal, providing this kind of structure usually keeps the teacher in control of unwanted movement patterns, which can interfere with the learning of many other students.

Provide definable boundaries. Younger AD/HD students who must move about frequently may benefit from having a specified area for their movement. With the student's input, a teacher can mark an area in which movement is permitted. When the student needs to get up and move, he or she is to remain within the identified boundary. Masking tape can usually be used to create an area around the student or within the classroom. Unfortunately, some teachers abuse this technique by creating an extremely small area, which becomes more of a "jail" than a "yard." The idea is to expand rather than contract the available, legitimate space the child has to move in so that others are undisturbed while the child meets his or her need for movement.

Legitimize the behavior with limits to teach impulse control. Impulse-control problems stem from the student's inability to monitor and control certain behaviors. When behaviors occur at a very high frequency with kids who seem driven to behave in that way, an effective strategy is to allow and even encourage behaviors that you want to reduce. When limits are placed on the frequency of a behavior rather than its occurrence, many students will actually seek greater self-control. The strategy involves identifying a finite number of times that the behavior will be acceptable with the student and then finding a way for the student to hold him- or herself accountable for keeping to the agreed-upon number.

For example, a student who taps a pencil endlessly can be asked, "How many times do you think you will absolutely need to tap your pencil during today's class, keeping in mind the needs of the other students?" If the student answers with a completely unacceptable number such as 100 or a million, the teacher challenges the student with an amount that the teacher can live with: "I can't teach and others can't learn when it happens all day, but I can probably live with somewhere between 8 and 10 pencil taps. What number will work for you?" When the student offers a number, he or she is given the same number of pencil-tap "coupons." If the student redeems all of the coupons, then no more of the behavior is permitted during the agreed-on duration.

This technique can be applied to all behaviors that happen excessively but are neither dangerous nor unsanitary. Variations can be adapted at all ages. These methods provide opportunities for students with impulse-control problems to monitor themselves. For example, a younger student can be given a smiley face chart and told to put a sticker in a box under a smiley face each time he thinks he is going to have to break a rule but does not, and a mark in a box under the frowning face each time he breaks the rule but stops misbehaving before being told to do so by an adult. The goal is for the student to achieve more successes while developing a more stop-and-think approach. An older student who "cuts up" in class can be challenged as follows: "Lou, you're funny, and that helps keep us all in a good mood. But sometimes it gets out of hand and gets in the way of learning. So how many jokes do you think you'll need to tell today? Let's figure out the best times to tell them."

When a student repeats the target behavior after the limit has been reached, gentle coaxing will be more effective than a reprimand. It is not helpful to say, "Lou, you agreed on five times, but now you've done it six times. That's a detention." It is better to offer, "Lou, I see how hard you are trying, but you have no more cards left. I know you can wait until tomorrow when you have more cards. I appreciate that." Keep in mind that these impulse-control techniques are designed for the student who is not malicious, but does have control problems. They do not work as well with "belligerent" students who are intent on having a power struggle for purposes of being in control. If you are unsure how well this strategy would work with a student, try it five times. If the student's behavior does not improve, move on.

Do not hassle over supplies. AD/HD students are notoriously forgetful about all things unrelated to their interests and often show up with the wrong book, if any, and no paper or necessary supplies. As often as possible, educators should provide duplicate supplies and materials without worrying about encouraging these students to become irresponsible. Instead, focus on teaching them to put their things in the same place every time. Cigar and shoeboxes can be helpful. Give them checklists and go over them orally for a week or two before asking these students to use them by themselves. Many power struggles and lost learning opportunities occur because of poor preparation by students. Rather than struggle with these students over these issues, it is much better to encourage all students to contribute supplies as needed. With an abundance of necessary supplies contributed by peers, the student's forgetful behavior can become an opportunity for him or her to simply get the needed material, taking little or no time away from learning. Most schools have a never-ending supply of pencils on the floor. Sending out a pencil-scouting patrol of AD/HD students who need to move can turn up all the pencils a class will ever need. Students are encouraged to contribute supplies after "borrowing," and donations are solicited when necessary.

Use small, furry animals. Petting animals can often have a calming effect on jittery students. Naturally, the educator needs to be sensitive to other students who might be allergic and to school or health policies that may limit or forbid animals in school. But for some students, petting a small furry animal for at least 20 minutes can have the same result, through a different psychochemical brain reaction, as Ritalin. Birds, fish, and reptiles do not work.

Provide fidgeting supports. AD/HD students are often excessively fidgety. They may knock against their desks, drum with their fingers, and tap their pencils. This distracts others from learning and the teacher from teaching. Providing a small rubber square or a mouse pad can allow for muffled "pencil-tapping" and "drum-rolling" so that others are not distracted. Providing a Koosh ball or other stress-squeezing object can allow for safe, silent hand movement.

Give one step at a time. When giving directions, giving them one step at a time is most likely to yield compliance. For example, students are first told the directions to an assignment. Then one or more are asked to repeat back what is expected. The next step may be to ask students to take out a pencil. Finally, ask students to do the assignment. Many AD/HD students cannot handle doing several things simultaneously (nor can many people never diagnosed with AD/HD). Expecting them to listen while writing can be a disaster. You will often achieve better results by limiting these students to one aspect of a task at a time.

Believe that small success is better than large failure. AD/HD students need teachers who are good at reframing situations. Teachers who view them as already having the strengths they need, but not yet being able to apply those strengths consistently, usually elicit better results because their approach reduces the likelihood of power struggles around behaviors of noncompliance. Since it is the rare AD/HD student who "never" engages in the desirable behavior, it is affirming to these students when they realize that they already have the necessary skills but simply need to apply them in other ways. For example, after sitting and attending for five minutes to a story, it is affirming and skill-building to approach the AD/HD student and say, "Paul, you just got through the last five minutes in your seat and when you went to sharpen your pencil, you got to the pencil sharpener without bumping anybody. Did you notice that? How were you able to make that happen? Let's learn from today because we both now know that there are times when you can do it!"

Encourage students to exercise. Considerable data point to the benefits that exercise has on attending and learning. Allen (1980) and Bass (1985) found that running improved attention span and impulse-control while reducing disruptions by 50%. Shipman (1985) found that jogging decreased hyperactivity and impulsivity. Students who were taking stimulant medication required less medication when they were jogging regularly. Exercise was found to have its best effects during the first two to four hours after jogging. Putnam and Copans (1998) write that there are even significant data to suggest that periods of regular exercise, every two to four hours, might lead to improvements in the ability of AD/HD children to function.

Encourage mental relaxation. Our experience with AD/HD students suggests that most can benefit from basic methods of relaxation such as repetitive counting, deep breathing for a few minutes while thinking of a sound or word, and listening to relaxation tapes. Our earlier work offers many suggestions for blending these strategies within the classroom (Curwin & Mendler, 1997; Mendler, 1990).

GANGS

Gangs exist because they meet basic needs. They are family to those who have none, or none that functions in a familial way. They are structured groups with an identifiable hierarchy that welcome children and help them feel capable and powerful. Paradoxically, although children in gangs often engage in dangerous activities, most of them feel safe and protected by their gang. Once a child joins a gang, it is very difficult to lure him or her away. Children often become involved in gangs gradually. Without fully intending to join, they may first do "little" things like stealing at the urging of a friend or sibling. Before long, these children want to be full-fledged members and will "pay" to become members by being "beat in," "sexed in," or "crimed in."

A student's gang activity ends only when there is another place to go that offers connectedness, safety, respect, influence, and stimulation. Unfortunately, many do not leave gangs even when they want to because they fear injury or even death. Efforts to counteract the influence of gangs need to include multidisciplinary interventions that involve parents, courts, police, the community, and schools. Sadly, not enough students view school as a viable alternative to the gang even though, theoretically, school can be a very strong alternative. Changing this reality is not easy, but caring educators can use a number of strategies to make a difference and influence change.

Meet basic needs. As mentioned earlier, several educators and psychologists have noted how unmet basic human needs often lead to maladaptive behavior. Although the names and descriptions of these basic needs vary, it is clear that healthy development is facilitated by people who give us a sense of belonging. Children who feel disconnected from others can create serious problems for themselves and everyone around them. Conversely, students are more likely to view school favorably when the school offers mentoring programs and has teachers who warmly greet children; show caring; ask, "What's happening?"; and offer support when a student is having a bad day. To compete successfully with gangs, our classrooms must be places where reasonable student effort results in successful achievement. As we stated in Chapter 1, all effort must count, and no effort should be ignored.

Do not allow gangs to represent at school. A school and its staff must learn the various dress and symbols used by local gangs so that the staff can take steps to prevent students from using or wearing those symbols at school. Having discussions with gang leaders, in which behavior and dress limits are explained, will usually lead to respect and compliance. However, when gangs are a major presence on campus, the school should seriously consider adopting a specific dress code or requiring student uniforms.

Be vigilant in enforcing violations of law. Students must know that the adults around them will protect their safety.

Violations of law, such as the presence of weapons and/or the use of drugs, must be vigorously pursued. School staff must be brave, assertive, and insistent while confronting behaviors that would destroy the learning climate for students and staff morale. Huff (1990) has noted that teachers who demonstrate that they care but are firm and fair in their expectations are rarely, if ever, assaulted.

Identify school or community service projects that need student involvement. One of the best ways to promote cooperation is to identify projects that benefit a targeted group (e.g., senior citizens or disabled children) and encourage gangs to join together in sponsoring activities to complete the project. Some staff may be reluctant to encourage these kinds of initiatives for fear that they are sanctioning the gangs' existence. In fact, we are best able to help students change their behavior when we bring them closer to us. Acknowledging that gangs exist and then providing a positive, alternative activity involving all gang members is a powerful way of accepting the choices students have made in the past while encouraging them to make better, different choices in the future.

Show respect. Because the two constant, primary objectives of gang members are maintaining the respect of peers and maintaining their own self-respect, you should avoid threatening students who belong to gangs. Most gang members feel powerful and invulnerable, and are hypersensitive to public displays of criticism and humiliation. Threats of disciplinary action often spark power struggles. Any concerns you have about them or their behavior should be shared with them privately to allow them choices that enable them to save face. Gang members are likely to view a teacher who humiliates them as an enemy and to desire revenge for the loss of face.

Meet with gang leaders when you need to set limits or defuse tensions. Children in gangs crave respect and want influence. Interestingly, these children and their leaders are often quite responsible when given opportunities to be in charge. It is wise to include them in school decision-making activities that are supervised. For example, include them on school committees that are exploring ways of making the school a better place. The participation and involvement of students who are causing problems often aid important initiatives such as improving school climate and making discipline more effective. Their proposed solutions are often the most effective because of their close proximity to the problems.

Have periodic "sweeps" to monitor controlled substances. The school must be a safe place. All students need to know that the adults in their school are serious about ensuring an environment that supports learning. Staff visibility in the halls and other places in which students congregate is very important. It is also appropriate to do sweeps in collaboration with the police when drug use and/or possession is suspected.

Gangs are a fact of life in the United States, existing not only in large, urban areas but also in small towns like Rapid City, South Dakota (Curwin & Mendler, 1997), and even Cozad, Nebraska. We can significantly reduce the dangerous, negative impact of gangs by containing their influence, providing alternative ways for students to meet their needs, setting limits, and refocusing student activities.

In this chapter, we have examined three special problems that most educators face: lack of student motivation, inattentive students, and student involvement in gangs. To handle these problems effectively, we need to look beyond the symptomatic behavior and consider the underlying causes of it. When we understand the motivation and needs of each individual student, we are more likely to find reasonable solutions to the challenges they present. All students need to be treated with respect and dignity and need to be seen as learners. If we categorize them as unteachable or unreachable, we are doomed to punish rather than help them, and our attempts will ultimately fail. The strategies and techniques in this chapter will help us respond to the challenges of these problems with greater success.

Frequently Asked Questions

Remorse without resolution and reparation is inadequate.

W HEN MOST EDUCATORS ask us questions about discipline, they are looking for specific strategies and how-to advice. Most of this book addresses important concepts relating to discipline and responsibility and includes many practical methods of prevention and intervention. Throughout this book, we have stressed our belief that there are no simple formulas for understanding the complexity of human behavior and there are no one-size-fits-all approaches to improving it. However, there are many specific strategies within the guidelines we have presented that will help educators solve some of the difficult issues we face. This chapter provides guidance on 10 of the questions we are asked most frequently by educators who work with difficult youth.

Q: My frustration as a special education teacher is that while my students make good progress in my resource classroom, many of them have difficulty adjusting to mainstream classes. Those teachers constantly complain about how irresponsible the kids are, and the kids are always complaining about how unfair the teachers are. Any suggestions?

A: Your students probably lack the social skills that would otherwise enable them to adjust to teachers who are less inclined than you are to consider the individual behind the behavior and try to meet the student's specific needs. Many special education students who are successful in resource or self-contained programs have acquired adequate academic skills but remain deficient in organizational and social skills. Look for ways to help them stay organized, a trait that many regular education teachers admire. Teach them the specific organizational skills that are likely to help them meet the regular education teacher's expectations and lead to success. Naturally, you will need to be in close contact with your regular education colleagues so that you understand their expectations.

You can also teach your students how to get along with these teachers by talking both formally and informally with the students to find out their teachers' needs and procedures. We have found that most students can easily learn and apply basic principles of positive social interaction, and can actually influence their teachers' behaviors by practicing and using them. For example, you can challenge your students to say "good morning" while making eye contact with the teacher as they enter the room. Point out that teachers appreciate students who sit up straight, lean forward, have a friendly smile, and show interest. Encourage them to raise their hand at least once each period to ask or answer a question. Have them be sure that their home-work is turned in on time. Special education teachers tend to "cut" their students more breaks, and the regular education teacher may resent that.

Finally, you might be in a good position to offer suggestions and effective strategies to your regular education colleagues. When you know or suspect that the teacher's behavior is triggering a negative student response, try to gently intervene during one of your monitoring or feedback sessions. You might say something like this: "Jarrel can be quite a handful when he doesn't get his way. He and I continue to work on finding better ways to handle his frustrations. In a class your size, I can appreciate how hard it can be to take time to calm him down when he gets overwhelmed, and I can certainly understand that there are times that you just can't be bothered. In case it helps, I have found that he reacts best when I correct him by _____ (offer the strategy or approach you'd like this colleague to emulate) and worst when I _____ (share an example of something similar to what this teacher is doing that you think is triggering the problem behavior). Is this something that might make sense for you to try with him in your classroom?" End by offering future support to your colleague (e.g., "How about if I touch base with you next week or sooner so that we can see if there has been any improvement?").

This example illustrates a helpful strategy you can use when providing feedback to regular education colleagues. You can:

1. Acknowledge how difficult the student can be.

2. Affirm how much more difficult the student's behavior is likely to be in a more "normal" setting.

3. Offer your own experience as to what you find effective and ineffective.

4. Encourage the colleague to use the effective approach or a close variation.

5. Make yourself available for a specific future consultation.

Q: Bullying is a big problem, even though only a few kids can really be considered to be bullies. Yet the fear and intimidation felt by others interfere with the school climate and student learning. Shouldn't these kids be suspended or perhaps put in alternative schools so that they do not adversely affect others?

A: Bullying is indeed a substantial problem for many children. The National Association of School Psychologists estimates that 160,000 children miss school every day for fear of being bullied. Often defiant and impulsive as well as popular, bullies show little concern for others and are more apt to misinterpret the actions and words of others as hostile. Bullies often have otherwise harmless "lieutenants" who participate in harassing behavior when the main bully is present. Interventions with bullies include confronting them and giving consequences that require some form of restitution, preferably to the school, such as cleaning the lunchroom or repairing or replacing broken property. We advise a stern, no-nonsense confrontation as quickly after an incident as possible. At the same time, since bullies have an excessive, misdirected need for power, you can also help them improve their behavior by redirecting and rechanneling their power in healthy ways. Possibilities include assigning them to safety patrol or making them bus monitors or lunchroom assistants.

Some bullies act out in response to anger, lack of attention, and being bullied at home. You do not need to become a psychologist or family intervention specialist to help bullies by teaching them other ways to resolve their frustrations. For example: "I noticed that sometimes you get frustrated and take it out on your classmates. Instead of hurting them, I bet you didn't realize that there are a lot of ways you can help them by _____ (offer suggestions). You will feel better, and others will start looking up to you. Think about it, and we'll talk later."

You can also teach potential victims of bullying a number of strategies to reduce or stop the harassment. A school that mobilizes its energies to teach children to look after and support each other will provide its students with strength in numbers and reduce bullying behavior. Preventive efforts can include "No Bullying" campaigns supported by discussions, posters, and plays. Children who are new to the school or those considered at highest risk of being victimized can be paired with groups of strong students who can provide mentoring. Potential victims should be encouraged to avoid being alone with a bully.

Finally, we must teach all students skills for defusing confrontations to prevent them from being victimized by bullies. Students can be taught to use:

- Assertive strategies such as "I-messages"

- Calming strategies that help them stop and think when in a stressful situation

- Agreeing strategies (e.g., telling the bully: "You're right. I wish I had clothes as nice as yours.")

- Humor

- Avoidance (simply walking away)

We have found that most students need to learn and practice these skills before they can use them in actual bullying situations. Students can often identify other possible solutions when the problem of bullying is brought to their attention.

Q: Do you have any advice on making in-school suspension more effective? The same kids keep coming back. Right now we keep the students working in isolation. They must sit down and be quiet.

A: The rules you have in your in-school suspension are typical and generally work only for students who occasionally or rarely misbehave. Students who occasionally misbehave prefer spending their time someplace else doing something else, so using isolation as a deterrent for these students is often effective. Unfortunately, the same process is entirely ineffective for students who are frequently referred for in-school suspension. These students usually have significant problems in their lives, which fuel anger that leads to disruptive behavior and eventual referral. For them, even the threat of isolation is often not a powerful enough deterrent to keep their anger from erupting in inappropriate ways. A more effective approach suggested by Gootman (1998) is to borrow from the research on resilience, which finds that resilient students need three factors:

1. A relationship with an adult who thinks they are worthwhile.

2. Sensitivity to their feelings.

3. A sense of power and control in their lives.

The in-school suspension should be enforced in a place where students reflect on what they did by discussing it with a caring adult. Since most students believe that they are being unfairly treated, it can help to defuse those feelings by simply using reflective listening (e.g., "It must be difficult to believe that you are trying hard and not getting noticed" or "It is hard to sit still in class when there are so many other things on your mind"). Once the student is calmer and has been understood, the student and adult can begin to solve the problem. The adult can help the student develop a workable plan that will help solve the problem within the student's real world. For example: "Let's figure out how you can stay in your seat when there are so many things on your mind." The major emphasis of in-school suspension should be on teaching students more appropriate, adaptive behavior rather than on hoping that their misery will make them see the error of their ways. The adult in charge must be able to firmly and clearly tell the student that his or her behavior had a negative impact on others, while at the same time showing the student dignity and respect.

Unfortunately, in-school suspension rooms are often staffed by teachers who have little experience with such problem-solving methods and/or have far too many students to supervise for them to personally interact with each student. Administrators should do whatever is possible to reduce the number of referrals so that the process has a chance for success. Teachers with the right match of skills can be assigned to supervise suspended students and should be given a reduction in their other responsibilities to compensate.

One alternative to in-school suspension rooms is to remove a student from one class and send him or her to another classroom for a temporary out-of-class timeout without requiring a formal referral. The new teacher has no responsibility for handling the problem. The teacher only needs to provide a space for the student. This strategy is very successful and can dramatically reduce the number of students in in-school suspension. If in-school suspension continues to be a holding tank, its results are predictable—failure.

Q: My biggest problem is parents who will not accept that their child has problems. One child was recently recommended to be evaluated for medication, but his parents refused. What can be done?

A: Challenging parents can be more frustrating than their children. It helps to realize that even when we disagree with them, the fact that they are arguing with us or actively refusing our advice shows that they care about their child. After all, they could make themselves completely unavailable. However confrontational they are, it is important that we begin our side of any conference by sharing our appreciation for their involvement. Let them know that your only desire is to help their child learn responsibility and be successful. Remain open-minded to any suggestions they offer for helping you work more effectively with their child. If they suggest that you do something that you cannot (e.g., spank), let them know that doing what they ask at school is not an option and tell them why.

If parents completely refuse recommended treatment when their child's behavior is disrupting the learning process, we believe it is appropriate to offer home instruction. Unreasonable parents cannot be permitted to alter the learning experience of the other students. If you need to recommend home instruction, we suggest you do so in collaboration with your principal and possibly other support professionals, who can meet with the parents as a team to let them know that unless or until they provide the suggested treatment or offer an acceptable alternative, their child's education will be offered at home. If this is not possible, then explore the possibility of placing the child in an alternative setting. School districts are increasingly threatened with lawsuits, but must not back down when it is clear that a parent's decisions or demands create unsound conditions for student learning or safety.

Although many parents can be overbearing in defending their children's indefensible behavior, alternatives to such direct confrontation should not be used except in extreme cases. The techniques described earlier for defusing power struggles can be adapted for and made effective with parents. When the child is from a two-parent family, try to have both parents present at all discussions so one does not undermine the other at home. Start by assuming that all parents love their children. Search for common ground on what is wonderful and good about their child. Inquire about problems they face at home with the child and ask what works successfully for them. Share frustrations you have in common with your own children (or brothers and sisters when growing up). Finally, seek their suggestions for you while clearly and firmly defining your limits. Agree with what you can, and reject the rest in a kind but firm manner.

Q: I work with teenagers who have been to court. As a condition of their probation, judges often mandate that these students attend school. Most come but do nothing while they are here. They make it clear that they are here because they have to be. I feel like I am doing little more than babysitting or, in some cases, acting as a prison guard. Any suggestions?

A: When the court orders a youth to attend school as an alternative to incarceration, it is using the tool of leverage. We have found that requiring school attendance is usually an insufficient condition of probation. There is little reason to believe that schools are any more effective after a youth has been ordered to attend than they were before the court made its ruling. Therefore, specific academic requirements (e.g., attend class, do homework, maintain passing grades) and behavioral expectations (e.g., come to class on time) are needed in order to increase the likelihood that school attendance becomes a viable alternative. The youth should also know the specific people and places he or she can go to for help or to let off steam. Schools and courts work together most effectively when they collaborate along with the student and the family on a plan of improvement. This plan needs to include specific behavioral and academic expectations that are considered minimally acceptable. There should be regularly scheduled progress reviews and a process for assembling the concerned parties when problems occur.

Once these students are in class, our goal is for them to learn. Persuasion rarely works. Using motivation and welcoming strategies works best.

Q: Most students in my class are very nice when I talk to them individually about their behavior. But when they are together, it is common for one to start acting up, and then another one gets silly, and pretty soon I've got rowdy behavior with students playing off each other. Responding to this takes a lot of instructional time that would be much better spent learning. What else can I do?

A: There are many things to do for prevention and, when necessary, intervention. Preventing this problem is best accomplished by establishing rules with the students based on the value of respect. If students break the rules, you can schedule a planning session in which specific ways of solving the problem are explored. This is usually best done with a "ringleader" or with the small groups of students who are most often involved. If the problem persists, call home and discuss your concerns directly and privately with the student so you can elicit a specific commitment for changed behavior.

Students who regularly "get things going" have excessive needs for belonging, attention, and sometimes power. You might explore leadership opportunities in your classroom for them so they can be "in charge" while contributing to the well-being of the class. Another option is to set aside a few minutes for students to be silly and playful in nonoffensive ways. We recently visited a school in which the principal strongly encouraged the teaching staff to have "laughing time" in their classes. Two o'clock each day for two minutes was identified as laughing time at school. A bell rang to signal the beginning and end.

There may also be times when you need a break from one or more students who need excessive attention. Work out arrangements with fellow teachers or an administrator, or use a timeout for this purpose.

Q: I'm a secondary school teacher. Many of my colleagues and I have problems with disrespectful students we encounter outside of the classroom in common areas: the halls, cafeteria, or in front of the school. It is tempting to just look the other way and not be bothered because it is just such a no-win situation, but I keep telling myself that there needs to be a better way. Is there?

A: First of all, we applaud you for being outside of the classroom and considering it to be territory worthy of your attention and concern. We have found that when all or most staff are visible throughout the building, it is harder for difficult students to get into trouble because they have a greater sense of accountability, while students who do not get into trouble feel safer. In fact, many schools we have consulted with have found significantly improved behavior just by having its staff make a determined effort to be more visible.

When disrespectful behavior occurs, accountability and safety are the primary concerns. You do not want to endanger yourself or others by confronting students who may be volatile, but you do want to handle the student and his or her behavior so that the student and others understand that there are limits. It is usually best to avoid confronting the student when he or she appears to be emotionally aroused or hostile and responds disrespectfully to you. Find out who the student is and complete an incident report. It can be very effective to call this student at home later to convey your concern. For example: "Carla, this is Mr. Lee. I was in the hall this morning when you said or did _____. I'm sure you were upset about something, but I'm calling to tell you that when you do stuff like _____, it is embarrassing and unacceptable. I filled out an incident report because it is obviously against the rules to do _____, but more importantly, I want to let you know directly of my concern. Was there something I said or did that made you upset, or were you just blowing off steam? . . . I look forward to receiving your cooperation. Thanks."

There are many, less emotional situations when you can confront the student immediately. There does not have to be a big fuss. You should focus on doing something that makes it less likely for this student to repeat his or her behavior. For example, if you ask students to move along, and one says or does something that you find offensive and continues to walk away, go to the student or call a name (make one up if necessary). When the student turns around and corrects you for calling the wrong name, make a brief, clear, and respectful comment. For example, make eye contact and assertively say, "I'm sure you don't like to be hassled and neither do I. I won't hassle you when you don't hassle me. Thanks for following the rules when you walk down this hallway." Turn slowly and walk away.

In common areas, students often feel safer from being challenged because they feel they are more anonymous. Another way of getting the attention of an offending student when you do not know the student's name is by asking students nearby. This implicitly lets the student know that you know who he or she is.

Q: I cannot believe how angry more and more of my students are at younger and younger ages. What in the world is going on, and how can educators be expected to teach them reading when all they want to do is fight, argue, and talk tough, even to me?

A: As we stated in our book *As Tough as Necessary* (1997), there are more angry children today doing worse things at younger ages than ever before. Many of these angry children experience little or no remorse. The complex reasons for this include many familial, social, and neurological factors. For example, children born with fetal alcohol syndrome or addicted to crack often have a much lower ability to handle frustration, pay attention, and concentrate. They are also more likely to be living with a single parent, who is herself often overwhelmed by life's demands and who is less capable of modeling socially appropriate behavior. Angry kids with a low tolerance for frustration usually need established routines that are structured, predictable, clearly defined, and, in extreme cases, constant.

Because of the many complex factors that lead to maladaptive behavior, a significant commitment of time, attention, energy, and resources is necessary to teach these students healthy ways to express their anger without turning to harmful behavior. The growth of "violence prevention" curricula that emphasize teaching students social skills, stop-and-think strategies, and other ways of calming down have become necessary because too many students lack these basic skills. Educators also need to practice and model these strategies in order for students to begin using them during times of stress. We understand that all of this takes instructional time, but unless teachers use these strategies, they cannot expect their students to do so.

Q: Several other teachers and I want to change the way we discipline children in our school. However, there are many resistant, vocal faculty members with a significant amount of influence who not only resist change, but belittle it. What can we do?

A: All schools have some teachers who are cynical about challenging students. These students are often difficult to like, take a lot of time, and make us feel like failures. It is not difficult to understand why many teachers have even given up hope for improving these students' behavior. Chapters 3 and 4 ("Change Starts Within" and "Attitudes and Beliefs") offer many suggestions for helping us develop or reclaim the essential attitudes necessary for working effectively with challenging students. We must each fight the cynical voices from within that say, "That kid'll never make it," "What a waste of time and energy," or "Look at that family—there's no use!" because we can never influence change from a position of cynicism. While these cynical attitudes and behaviors are understandable, they can be dangerous for fellow faculty members and students by undermining the power of caring and collaboration. No students—especially challenging ones—should be taught by teachers who have given up hope.

The entire school must make a commitment to fight cynicism and keep the spirit of hope alive. An administrator can have cynical faculty members serve as chairpersons of committees that focus on change efforts for the same reasons we would assign responsible jobs to difficult students. Ask these teachers to look for problems in any new program to help make it more effective. In that way, their critical abilities can be put to a positive use. When you hear a cynical remark, you might courageously confront the speaker by saying, "That almost sounded cynical. I know you did not mean it that way, but someone might misinterpret your meaning. Just a friendly reminder to be more careful."

Finally, try to build a core of strong, positive teachers who meet and support each other regularly. Try to expand your group over time until it becomes a majority, whose actions speak louder than the cynical inaction of others and whose successes become an example to every other teacher in the school.

Q: Do all teachers have to discipline students consistently?

A: There are two types of consistency: internal and external. External consistency requires that all teachers use the same practices in their classrooms. This requirement is neither practical nor essential. There are individual differences in the ways we arrange our classrooms for instruction. Requiring the use of the same classroom rules and consequences is not essential to a healthy school. Children can learn many systems of discipline from an early age; they may know two by age two—their mother's and father's. Most important, the rules should be connected to values, and the consequences should be designed to teach improved behavior.

However, external consistency in the enforcement of school rules by everyone without regard to personal preference is necessary in the school's common areas (i.e., playground, cafeteria, hallways) to ensure orderliness. Students and educators benefit from school rules when they all work together towards a common purpose. It takes commitment and vision on the part of the faculty and administration to ensure that everyone follows the plan.

Internal consistency means that you follow and enforce your classroom rules. This is very important and necessary. Internal consistency is essential within the classroom to ensure that the classroom rules that were developed by the teacher and students are honored and enforced whenever they are broken.

Q: Is it helpful to discipline students in front of the whole class so others can see what happens to students who break the rules?

A: No, it is not. What students learn is that anyone, even themselves, may be ridiculed for making a mistake in your class. That lesson will undermine a productive learning atmosphere.

In addition, the student who is publicly disciplined might feel the need to defend him- or herself because of the audience, which most likely will lead to a power struggle and make matters worse. It is enough for other students to see the misbehavior stop. A far more important public lesson to give is that everyone, even those who make mistakes, has dignity, and that respecting that dignity matters to you. The social lesson of treating people with dignity far outweighs any possible advantage of making a public display of discipline.

Occasionally, a student's behavior makes private discipline impossible. In these cases, keep the interaction short, minimize humiliation, and talk with the student later in more detail. This book includes a number of scenarios that show how we can discipline in public while maintaining our dignity and the student's dignity. While private discipline is usually best, having to discipline a student in front of an audience provides an opportunity to model methods of communication that can effectively defuse power struggles. The student's dignity is honored, and other students see a valuable strategy in action.

Q: After making significant strides to improve my techniques, I have found myself gradually returning to old, ineffective ways of disciplining. It seems that the entire school reverts to old ways like I do even though we are enthusiastic about using new techniques that preserve a student's dignity. How can we maintain our progress?

A: Change is slow and is often difficult and frustrating. You and your colleagues are facing the same regression that students often do, described in Chapter 2, "The First 'R.'" Regressions are a natural part of the change process. They can be a temporary setback or a more permanent retreat from progress, depending on how we interpret and handle them.

Begin by developing a support group among your friends on the faculty that meets regularly. A support group of your colleagues will give you opportunities to keep working on issues that can make a difference with your students. It can also provide needed encouragement when you find yourself retreating to more familiar and less effective discipline techniques.

Keep a simple, informal record of what techniques are or are not working for you. Identify what feels good to do and what does not. Review your record from time to time to keep your enthusiasm high. Set new goals for yourself when other goals are met. For example, if you successfully master the art of private discipline, try learning how to reduce power struggles. Continuing to strive for new goals will greatly reduce complacency and the temptation to regress. But try not to take on too much at any one time or you will feel that the peak of the mountain you are trying to climb is always out of reach. Small steps are easier to take than large ones.

Finally, challenge your administrator(s) to make discipline and improvement a continuous, high priority both in terms of individual teachers and the school as a whole. It might even become part of the assessment sequence. Faculty meetings might include anecdotal reporting of both successes and difficulties for all to share and consider possible solutions.

10

Worth the Struggle

In the end, test scores do nothing to improve a student's character. That is determined by how responsible he or she is.

S UCCESS WITH CHALLENGING students requires knowledgeable, caring adults who refuse to reject them even when they behave in offensive, obstinate, defiant, unmotivated, and hostile ways. We must make it difficult for students to throw away their education and their lives. We must find ways of seeing past their behavior so that who they are is more important than what they do. They need us to believe in them and give them hope so they can believe in themselves.

We are more successful when we thank challenging students for giving us an opportunity to learn and grow in our own quest to become great teachers. For while the best students will reinforce us to stay the same, because what we do appears to work, the most difficult students force us to see clearly what does not work and motivate us to find what does. As we meet these challenges, all students benefit, even the best, because we have made their learning environment safer. We have also made it easier for our students to learn, because the new skills we learn when we work with difficult students make us more attuned to the needs of all of our students and better able to teach them.

We hope you have found helpful, practical strategies and inspiration as you have read these pages. We believe that the many proven ideas in this book will help you teach your challenging students to become more responsible, set limits more clearly, and handle power struggles more effectively. But most importantly, we want to assure you that major victories are achieved in small, sometimes imperceptible, steps. Regressions should not be viewed as failure but as a normal part of the many day-to-day battles you will wage with your challenging students. On behalf of the many disconnected, troubled students you see each day, we want to thank you for the time and energy you have committed to giving them hope. Your students and their parents may never truly understand what it takes to make a difference, but we do.

We end with a poem written by Kareem—a teen-aged, court-adjudicated resident of New York State—due to his juvenile delinquency. Kareem's words eloquently describe how we all need to work together when we truly want to influence change.

When I sleep, I dream of days
Of perfect days with nothing but sun,
Rainbows that end in a misty haze:
And all my people are forever one.
We're all united in an unbreakable chain
We know not the words hate and pain,
All we know is love and peace,
Beautiful things that would never cease;
Then there's a time when I awake and see
That none of that is reality;
And in order for all those things to be,
It's up to everyone:
You and me.

Appendix: Case Study—Niles Community Schools

The Niles Community Schools in Niles, Michigan, have developed a comprehensive discipline plan that includes values, rules, and consequences as suggested in Chapter 7, "Seven Goals for Successful Discipline." We thank Niles Community Schools for their permission to reprint the following documents from their discipline plan.

BEHAVIOR VISION

Our vision is a safe and secure environment in which the dignity of each individual is respected.

Our vision asserts that all will:

- Respect themselves and others.

- Act as responsible, productive citizens.

- Demonstrate the ability to problem solve, predict consequences, and make appropriate choices.

BACKGROUND AND RATIONALE

The student is the reason for our being. We know that our students have diverse backgrounds and needs. Our charge and challenge is to accept these differences and meet each student's needs as we educate the adult citizens of tomorrow.

The success of our students and indeed our school system is dependent on creating a safe and secure environment where the behavior of all is conducive to successful learning. The desire for a quality life in our schools and our community compels us to expect and teach our students to be reasonable, productive adult citizens.

The success of students today and in tomorrow's global society is directly related to their perception of self-worth; their interpersonal and intrapersonal skills; and their ability to problem solve, predict consequences, and make appropriate choices.

The Niles Community Schools recognizes that family involvement can help children achieve success in school. Each child's education is the shared responsibility of the school, the parent, and the student. Such a collaborative partnership can help motivate, support, and encourage the student.

IMPLEMENTATION

To advance our vision, the Niles Community Schools' staff, parents, and community must embrace and promote the vision.

To support and sustain the vision, the Niles Community Schools must:

1. Develop leaders within the school community.

2. Develop a dynamic framework of knowledge and skills.

3. Provide staff development programs.

4. Provide parent involvement and educational opportunities for parents.

5. Use appropriate assessment approaches to measure effectiveness and make adjustments.

6. Promote partnerships and coalitions within the school community and the community at large.

Within each school and classroom, we must set clear expectations for student behavior with a range of appropriate consequences. Every staff member must be a model of a responsible, productive citizen. Students must be given the knowledge and taught skills for becoming responsible, productive citizens. The dignity and self-worth of every individual in the school community must be promoted and respected.

GUIDING PRINCIPLES

Developing responsible, respectful, problem-solving citizens who are able to predict consequences and make wise behavior choices is one of the goals of educators.

We believe successful, productive, capable people possess:

- Positive perceptions of personal capabilities.

  "I am capable."

- Positive perceptions of significance in primary relationships.

  "I contribute in meaningful ways, and I am genuinely respected."

- Positive perceptions of personal power of influence over life.

  "I can influence what happens to me."

- Strong intrapersonal skills.

  The ability to understand personal emotions, use that understanding to develop self-discipline and self-control, and learn from experience.

- Strong interpersonal skills.

  The ability to work with others and develop friendships through communication, cooperation, negotiation, sharing, empathizing, and listening.

- Strong systemic skills.

  The ability to respond to the limits and consequences of everyday life with responsibility, adaptability, flexibility, and integrity.

- Strong judgment skills.

  The ability to use wisdom and evaluate situations according to appropriate values.

We believe:

- Behavior can be changed.
- Behavior can be taught.
- Behavior must be modeled.
- Behavior is a result of an individual responding to his or her environment to meet basic needs.
- Behavior is non-negotiable in instances of safety and security.
- Behavior has consequences.

We believe:

- Consequences should be fair and not always equal.

- Consequences teach about behavior.

- Consequences should not be punishments.

CODE OF CONDUCT

The primary objective of requiring appropriate student behavior and self-discipline is to produce a positive and safe learning atmosphere in which there will be no interruption of the teaching-learning environment. All students will assume personal responsibility for their behavior and actions, develop appropriate self-control, exhibit self-discipline, and accept the responsibility and consequences of any inappropriate behavior. To accomplish this objective requires a cooperative effort from students, staff, and parents.

All students shall:

- Respect the educational process through the display of appropriate language, attitude, and physical behavior.

- Respect and honor the rights of other students to learn in an environment free of intimidation or harassment.

- Maintain satisfactory attendance.

- Report to classes on time.

- Comply with the dress code.

Consequences for noncompliance for the above expectations shall include, but not be limited to, the list below. The severity or the repetitive nature of a student's behavior will be given consideration when determining appropriate consequences.

- Community or school service

- Detention

- Denial of participation in school activities
- Denial of privileges
- Intervention by professional school staff
- Parent contact or conference
- Referral to an administrative panel
- Referral to appropriate law enforcement or other governmental agency
- School probation
- Warnings

The following behaviors will be considered unacceptable by Niles Community Schools and will result in suspension and an administrative hearing. The behaviors listed below apply to actions on school property and school-sponsored activities.

- Any purposeful action that results in great bodily harm to another human being.
- Use or possession of a weapon, explosive, look-alike, or anything that is used as a weapon. (Possession means on self or school property.)
- Possession or use of any drugs or look-alikes (includes alcohol and tobacco).
- Physical assaults to any school staff or school representative (shoving, pushing, spitting, hitting, etc.).
- Acts of arson.
- Acts of stalking (repeated or continuing harassment of another individual that would cause a reasonable person to feel terrorized, frightened, intimidated, threatened, harassed, or molested).

Bibliography

Allen, J. I. (1980, Winter). Jogging can modify disruptive behaviors. *Teaching Exceptional Children*, 66–70.

American Psychological Association (1993). *Violence and youth: Psychology's response.* Volume I: Summary Report of the American Psychological Association Commission on Violence and Youth. Washington, DC: APA Public Interest Directorate.

Applestein, C. D. (1994). *The Gus chronicles.* Needham, MA: Albert E. Trieschman Center.

Armstrong, T. (1994). *Multiple intelligences in the classroom.* Alexandria, VA: Association for Supervision and Curriculum Development.

Armstrong, T. (1998). *Awakening genius.* Alexandria, VA: Association for Supervision and Curriculum Development.

Bass, C. K. (1985). Running can modify classroom behavior. *Journal of Learning Disabilities, 18*(3), 160–161.

Bleick, C. R., & Abrams, A. I. (1987). The transcendental meditation program and criminal recidivism in California. *Journal of Criminal Justice, 15*(3), 211–230.

Brendtro, L., Brokenleg, M., & Van Bockern, S. (1990). *Reclaiming youth at risk: Our hope for the future.* Bloomington, IN: National Educational Service.

Brown, W. (1983). *The other side of delinquency.* Piscataway, NJ: Rutgers University Press.

Brownlee, S. (1996). Invincible kids. *U.S. News & World Report, 121*(19), 63–73.

Caine, R. N., & Caine, G. (1991). *Making connections: Teaching and the human brain.* Alexandria, VA: Association for Supervision and Curriculum Development.

Canter, L., & Canter, M. (1997). *Lee Canter's assertive discipline: Positive behavior management for today's classroom,* 3rd ed. Santa Monica, CA: Lee Canter and Associates.

Carlson, R. (1997). *Don't sweat the small stuff.* New York: Hyperion.

Caspi, A. (1996). Reported in Burnette, E., & Murray, B., Conduct disorders need early treatment. *American Psychological Association Monitor, 27*(10), 53–55.

Csikszentmihalyi, M. F. (1990). *Flow: The psychology of optimal experience.* New York: Harper Perennial.

Curwin, R. (1990). *Developing responsibility and self-discipline.* Rochester, NY: Discipline Associates Press.

Curwin, R. (1992). *Rediscovering hope: Our greatest teaching strategy.* Bloomington, IN: National Educational Service.

Curwin, R., & Mendler, A. (1988). *Discipline with dignity.* Alexandria, VA: Association for Supervision and Curriculum Development.

Curwin, R., & Mendler, A. (1997). *As tough as necessary: A discipline with dignity approach to countering aggression, hostility, and violence.* Alexandria, VA: Association of Supervision and Curriculum Development.

Dobson, J. (1996). *The new dare to discipline.* Carol Stream, IL: Tyndale House Publishers.

Dreikurs, R. (1964). *Children: The challenge.* New York: Dutton.

Dunn, R., & Dunn, K. (1982). *Teaching students through their individual learning styles.* Reston, VA: Reston Publishing Company.

Eggert, L. L., & Long, N. (1994). *Anger management for youth: Stemming aggression and violence.* Bloomington, IN: National Educational Service.

Gardner, H. (1993). *Multiple intelligences: The theory in practice.* New York: Basic Books.

Garrity, C., Porter, W., & Jens, K. (1996). Quoted by N. Seppa in Keeping schoolyards safe from bullies. *American Psychological Association Monitor, 27*(10), 41.

Geller, E. S. (1996). *The psychology of safety: How to improve behavior and attitudes on the job.* Radnor, PA: Chilton.

Glasser, W. (1986). *Control theory in the classroom.* New York: Harper & Row.

Goldstein, A., & Glick, B. (1987). *Aggression replacement training.* Champaign, IL: Research Press.

Goodlad, J. I. (1984). *A place called school: Prospects for the future.* San Francisco: McGraw-Hill.

Goodlad, J. I. (1990). *Teachers for our nation's schools.* San Francisco: Jossey-Bass.

Gootman, M. (1998). Effective in-house suspension. *Educational Leadership, 56*(1), 39–41.

Gunnar, M. (1996). Quoted by S. Brownlee in Invincible Kids. *U.S. News & World Report, 121*(19), 72.

Herbst, D. (1996). Emotional healing for aggressive youth. *Reaching Today's Youth, 1*(1), 17–19.

Huff, C. R. (1990). *Gangs in America.* Newbury Park, CA: Sage.

Kohn, A. (1996). What to look for in a classroom. *Educational Leadership, 54*(1), 54–55.

Kraus, S. (1995). Students with emotional disabilities prove successful mediators. *School Violence Alert, 1*(3), 4–5.

Lambert, L. (1998). *Building leadership capacity in schools.* Alexandria, VA: Association for Supervision and Curriculum Development.

Lantieri, L., & Patti, J. (1996). *Waging peace in our schools.* Boston: Beacon Press.

Leo, J. (1996). Foul words, foul culture. *U.S. News & World Report, 120*(16), 73.

Long, N., & Morse, W. (1996). *Conflict in the classroom: The education of at-risk and troubled students.* Austin, TX: Pro-Ed.

Maslow, A. H. (1968). *Toward a psychology of being.* New York: Van Nostrand Reinhold.

Mendler, A. (1990). *Smiling at yourself.* Santa Cruz, CA: ETR Associates.

Mendler, A. (1992). *What do I do when...? How to achieve Discipline with Dignity in the classroom.* Bloomington IN: National Educational Service.

Mendler, A. (1997). *Power struggles.* Rochester, NY: Discipline Associates.

Philliber, S. (1995). *A "what works" report: Supporting effective youth development programs.* St. Louis: St. Louis Metropolitan Association for Philanthropy.

Prager, D. (1995). *Think a second time.* New York: HarperCollins.

Putnam, S., & Copans, S. A. (1998). Exercise: An alternative approach to the treatment of AD/HD. *Reaching Today's Youth, 2*(2), 66–68.

Quinn, P. E. (1984). *Cry out.* Nashville, TN: Abingdon Press.

Quinn, P. E. (1986). *Renegade saint.* Nashville, TN: Abingdon Press.

Rozman, D. (1994). *Meditating with children: The art of concentration and centering.* Boulder Creek, CA: Planetary Publications.

Rutstein, N. (1997). *Racism.* Washington, DC: The Global Classroom.

Sagor, R. (1996). Building resiliency in students. *Educational Leadership, 54*(1), 38–43.

Seita, J., Mitchell, M., & Tobin, C. (1996). *In whose best interest? One child's odyssey, a nation's responsibility.* Elizabethtown, PA: Continental Press.

Shipman, W. M. (1985). Emotional and behavioral effects of long-distance running on children. In M. L. Sachs & G. W. Buffone (Eds.), *Running as therapy* (pp. 125–127). Lincoln, NE: University of Nebraska Press.

Sparks, D., & Hirsh, S. (1997). *A new vision for staff development.* Alexandria, VA: Association for Supervision and Curriculum Development.

Sylwester, R. (1995). *A celebration of neurons: An educator's guide to the human brain.* Alexandria, VA: Association for Supervision and Curriculum Development.

Tierney J., Dowd, T., & O'Kane, S. (1993). Empowering aggressive youth to change. *Journal of Emotional and Behavioral Problems, 2*(1), 41–45.

USA Weekend (1996, September 6–8). What 222,653 teens said, 10.

Wlodkowski, R., & Ginsberg, M. (1995). *Diversity and motivation.* San Francisco: Jossey-Bass.

Wlodkowski, R., & Jarnes, J. (1990). *Eager to learn: Helping children become motivated and love learning.* San Francisco: Jossey-Bass.

Wood, M., & Long, N. (1991). *Life space intervention.* Austin, TX: Pro-Ed.

Wright, E. (1997). *The heart and wisdom of teaching.* San Francisco: Teaching from the Heart.

About *Discipline with Dignity for Challenging Youth* and the National Educational Service

The mission of the National Educational Service is to provide tested and proven resources that help those who work with youth create safe and caring schools, agencies, and communities where all children succeed. *Discipline with Dignity for Challenging Youth* is just one of many resources and staff development opportunities NES provides that focus on building a community circle of caring. If you have any questions, comments, articles, manuscripts, or youth art you would like us to consider for publication, please contact us at the address below. Or visit our website at:

www.nesonline.com

Staff Development Opportunities Include:

Improving Schools Through Quality Leadership
Integrating Technology Effectively
Creating Professional Learning Communities
Building Cultural Bridges
Discipline With Dignity
Ensuring Safe Schools
Managing Disruptive Behavior
Reclaiming Youth at Risk
Working With Today's Families

National Educational Service
304 W. Kirkwood Avenue, Suite 2
Bloomington, IN 47404-5132
(812) 336-7700
(800) 733-6786 (toll-free number)
FAX (812) 336-7790
e-mail: nes@nesonline.com
www.nesonline.com

NEED MORE COPIES OR ADDITIONAL
RESOURCES ON THIS TOPIC?

Need more copies of this book? Want your own copy? Need additional resources on this topic? If so, you can order additional materials by using this form or by calling us toll free at (800) 733-6786 or (812) 336-7700. Or you can order by FAX at (812) 336-7790, or visit our website at www.nesonline.com.

Title	Price*	Quantity	Total
Discipline with Dignity for Challenging Youth	$ 24.95		
As Tough as Necessary video training series	395.00		
What Do I Do When . . . ? How to Achieve Discipline with Dignity	21.95		
Rediscovering Hope: Our Greatest Teaching Strategy	21.95		
Discipline with Dignity video training series	356.00		
Power Struggles	11.95		
Anger Management for Youth: Stemming Aggression and Violence	24.95		
Teaching Self-Control	27.95		
An Educator's Legal Guide to Stress-Free Discipline and School Safety	79.00		
The Bullying Prevention Handbook	23.95		
		SUBTOTAL	
		SHIPPING	
Continental U.S.: Please add 5% of order total. Outside continental U.S.: Please add 7% of order total.			
		HANDLING	
Continental U.S.: Please add $3. Outside continental U.S.: Please add $5.			
		TOTAL (U.S. funds)	

*Price subject to change without notice.

❏ Check enclosed ❏ Purchase order enclosed
❏ Money order ❏ VISA, MasterCard, Discover, or American Express (circle one)

Credit Card No._____ Exp. Date_____
Cardholder Signature _____

SHIP TO:
First Name_____ Last Name_____
Position _____
Institution Name_____
Address_____
City_____ State_____ ZIP_____
Phone_____ FAX_____
E-mail _____

National Educational Service
304 W. Kirkwood Avenue, Suite 2
Bloomington, IN 47404-5132
(812) 336-7700 • (800) 733-6786 (toll-free number)
FAX (812) 336-7790
e-mail: nes@nesonline.com • www.nesonline.com